Future Pull

Partner with the Universe to Create the Life of Your Dreams

JACQUELINE GARWOOD

Sun Moon and Compass
149 Pine Street
Thunder Bay, Ontario
Canada P7A 5X4

Copyright © Jacqueline Garwood

All rights reserved. This book may not be reproduced in whole or in part, stored in a retrieval system, or transmitted in any form or by any means – electronic, mechanical, or other – without written permission from the publisher, except by a reviewer, who may quote brief passages in a review.

ISBN 978-0-9866808-4-7

Also by Jacqueline Garwood:

- Future Pull: Partner with the Universe to Create the Life of Your Dreams (First Edition)
- Future Pull: Life Creation Playbook and Journal
- The Seven Day Mental Diet: Updated for the 21st Century

Visit our website at: www.FuturePull.com or www.JacquelineGarwood.com

The Peony Nebula

*We come spinning out of nothingness,
scattering stars like dust*
-Rumi

If there was a Universal Olympics, the Peony nebula star would win the silver medal as the second brightest star in the galaxy. In my opinion, if there was a Universal beauty pageant, the Peony Nebula would win by a landslide.

The Peony Nebula, shown in the NASA image on the front cover and home of the Peony nebula star, is really just a cloud of dust, made visible through the miracle of infrared technology and the Spitzer Space Telescope.

The Peony nebula star shines with the equivalent light of 3.2 million suns.

Stars this massive are rare and puzzle astronomers because they push the limits required for stars to form.

The Peony star sheds an enormous amount of stellar matter in the form of strong winds. This matter is pushed so hard by strong radiation from the star that the winds speed up to about one million miles per hour in only a few hours. Ultimately, the Peony nebula star will live a short life of a few million years and will blow up in the most fantastic of cosmic explosions called a supernova.

Knowing that each of us, tiny humans on a tiny blue planet, are part of the great and awe-inspiring Universe, made up of the very same elements and connected at the most basic level, is a constant reminder that we are powerful partners with the Source of all that exists. It makes me feel both humble and powerful.

When we gaze up at the moon and stars and marvel at their beauty, we are catching a glimpse of our own divinity.

Dedicated to....

    This book is dedicated to you, the reader. You, along with my mentors both alive and dead, have been my teachers during the last quarter century that I have been leading visioning and goal setting workshops and exploring and fine-tuning the concepts contained in these pages.

    I would like to acknowledge the many people I talked to during the writing of this book who shared their experiences using the principles of Future Pull and the Law of Attraction. The many hours spent interviewing men and women who have been able to change their lives and achieve their dreams were truly transformative for me.

I also dedicate this to my son, John. You are the best example I know of someone who understands that you create your own reality and you do it masterfully.

And finally, I dedicate this to my grandson, Jack. You are the future.

How to Read This Book

*Man stands in his own shadow and
wonders why it's dark.*
-Zen Proverb

In the feng shui life path and career centre of my home, I have a tiny frame encasing a small piece of paper printed with my life purpose. It reads:

> "My purpose in this life is to help and inspire others to see the unlimited possibilities, to find their adventurous spirit and to walk their unique life path with joy and gratitude."

This book is intended first of all as an inspiration. I hope that you will see your future as one of unlimited possibility. If you do nothing more than read it through and begin to open yourself up to trying new things and walking new paths, my purpose will be fulfilled.

However, I also want to pass on to you my understanding of what works and what doesn't, based not only on personal trial and error but on the experiences of the many people who have participated in my workshops and retreats over the last thirty years.

In the summer of 2010, I interviewed people from around the world who were generous enough to share their stories and to reinforce or, in some cases, challenge, preconceived ideas. You'll find their stories scattered throughout this book.

This edition of Future Pull has a companion, *Future Pull Life Creation Playbook and Journal*. The Playbook and Journal is intended to serve as a guide to the application of the concepts presented in this book. The Playbook has action steps that, if taken, will help you apply the concepts in this book, from creating a compelling vision to walking the path into your ideal life. The Journal allows you to record your journey and contains reflection questions to encourage you to drill deeper, to deal with limiting thoughts, celebrate your progress, and appreciate your life now and your expansion into your future.

The Hermit card in the Tarot was my inspiration for the *Future Pull Life Creation Playbook and Journal.* The ninth card in the Major Arcana, the Hermit is pictured standing on the highest peak among the surrounding mountains. In his right hand he holds a lantern which appears to be lighting his way. Some see him as a wise man who wanders at night, lighting dark corners and looking for enlightenment. However, it can also be that the lantern's light is intended for seekers, others like you and I, who are still climbing and struggling up the mountainside below him. The Hermit is looking down, watching our progress.

According to Carl Jung he is really that part of us, the Divine within, that is ready to provide us direction and truth.

We have only to go within to ask for guidance.

So how should you read this book? There are no 'shoulds'. Read it as you wish. Read it through once and let it work its magic on a subconscious level as you start to try on new ways of thinking and behaving. Or take it a chapter at a time, reading and working through the Playbook and Journal.

You can also download 'Light Your Path' pages from the full-size version of this book at www.FuturePull.com. At the Future Pull website, you will also find other resources to help you drill deeper.

You might consider working through the book with a group of like-minded spiritual seekers. You are welcome to join one of the mastermind groups that are available through www.FuturePull.com. At the website you can sign up to receive notification of upcoming retreats or online workshops.

However you choose to proceed, my wish for you is that you let the ideas in this book lead you where you haven't been before. Step out of your box and expand your horizons. Your life will never be the same.

Contents

The Peony Nebula v
Dedicated to... vii
How to Read This Book ix

Introduction 1

Is This the Life You Were Born to Live? 13

MAKE THE CONNECTION

Make the Connection 19

Adopt a Perspective of
Unlimited Possibility 23

The Nature of Time 33

Future Pull 47

The Law of Attraction 55

The Importance of Gratitude 71

Recognize Your Power 77

Connect with the Universe 87

CREATE A COMPELLING VISION

Create a Compelling Vision   97
Start From Where You Are   101
Make Room for Your Future   107
Your Ideal Day   117
You May Be Closer Than You Think   131
Set Clear Intentions   135
A Visual Prayer   149
Choose Your Touchstone   159
Your Daily Practice   167

TAKE INSPIRED ACTION

Take Inspired Action   175
Take a Lesson from the Inch Worm   179
Serendipity and Synchronicity   191
Boost the Power of Future Pull   205
Chart Your Course   215

ALLOW THE UNIVERSE TO UNFOLD

Allow the Universe to Unfold   225
Let Go of the How's and When's   227

Give Up the Need to Know   235
Energy Soup   239
Guard Your Thoughts   249
Act As If   259
In the Meantime...   267

This is Just the Beginning   273
Resources   277
Acknowledgements   279
About the Author   283

Introduction

In the book of life, the answers aren't in the back.
-Charlie Brown

In 1981 I was a single mother; a high school dropout on welfare. Because I had an 'interesting' childhood—you know, the kind of 'interesting' that is intended in the Irish curse, "May you have an interesting life"—I was determined to give my son a better experience. I wanted him to have a stable childhood with friends he could keep for a lifetime, the opportunity to take part in sports and fun activities, a chance to finish school and the opportunity to become whatever he wanted to be.

I had gone to college as a mature student and, in spite of my conviction that I would never be able to compete with all those young high school graduates, I had graduated top of my class, winning the President's Medal. But disappointingly, my career had floundered at first. My job paid less than welfare. I had to work a lot of evenings and I just couldn't afford the day care. Life as a latchkey kid really wasn't what I had envisioned for my son. Two years after graduation, I was unemployed with absolutely no income—none at all for a period of time. I sold my furniture to buy food. It was deeply disappointing. I thought I was destined for a life on welfare in spite of my good intentions and hard work. But I still had my dreams and I persevered.

Then things started to take completely unexpected turns. As I had always wanted to be a writer, I entered a writer's contest sponsored by Chatelaine magazine. My entry had to be typewritten and I had no typewriter. I didn't even have a bed at that point. The local business supply store rented them out for the princely sum of $15.00 for the month—a fortune. I remember what a big decision that was—typewriter or food? I've always been good at convincing myself of the value of doing what I really want to do, whether it makes sense or not, so I rented the typewriter.

I typed out my story and submitted it and then had a brilliant idea. What if I put a sign up at the university to type student papers for $1.00 per page? Perhaps I could earn back what I had spent on renting the typewriter. Student typing was a big business back in the days before computers. Problem was, I really wasn't a very good typist and it was a basic typewriter without a self-correcting feature. No problem, I thought, I would use erasable paper.

My first customer was a forestry student with a seventy page essay—deadline Monday. It was Friday. That weekend there was a huge spring snowstorm. I sat on a hassock hunched over the coffee table day and night—as I said I wasn't a very good typist—and pecked that thing out. When he picked it up and gave me $70 cash I couldn't believe my good luck. I was rich! If we hadn't been snowed in we would have gone out for dinner and to a movie to celebrate.

Then I thought "Wow! If I got a better typewriter, one that was self-correcting, and did just one paper a week, I'd be rich!" I did some basic business research. In other words, I called the business supply company to see how much it cost to rent a fancy model with all the bells and whistles. And without any further thought or planning, I started my business. Within days I was the proud renter of a fancy Mastertype for $65 a month. Very scary! That was a lot of money. In fact that was about a third of my rent. I put signs up at the university and college and waited for the business to roll in. Nothing! Nada!

Now that I know better, I'm aware that I should have carried out some basic market research. Then I would have known that university was over and except for some summer essays and possibly a late doctoral thesis, there wasn't much call for student typists. Since then I've worked as a business consultant and taught small business start-up at the college, and I know that my story is a classic example of what not to do. But I've always enjoyed that old saying, "If you can't be a good example, you'll just have to be a horrible warning."

I didn't give up. I spent another $5–the constant outpouring of money was scary–and put an ad in the newspaper. I had a call! Someone wanted a resume typed. Of course I said yes, in spite of the fact that I had never had a resume and didn't know anything about them. But that's what we had libraries for, right? So I went to the library, took out every book on resumes and started working. It took me seven days to finish it and, because I used my $1 a page rate, I made $3. That obviously wasn't going to work.

I picked a number out of the air that seemed fair and raised my price for a resume to $21. I put another ad in the paper saying that I specialized in resumes. Specialized meant that I had done one and that I had a pile of books on how to write them. I started getting calls and the resumes started coming in.

It would literally take me up to a week to do one because I did so much research.

A year later I really was specializing in resumes and I was even getting some exposure as the local expert. I was being invited to speak to groups about how to write resumes. I had my package streamlined. I would interview clients—I called them clients by then, so much more professional—and then write and design unique resumes to suit their qualifications and career goals. I charged the exorbitant fee, in my mind, of $149. Wow! I really was rich! And I was a writer! And I had a bed!

By 1986, I had a flourishing business and I was starting to get enquiries to do training, not only on resume writing but on all things career-related. Of course, since I was skilled at 'acting as if', I never turned down an opportunity whether I knew anything about the subject or not. I would just say, "Sure. When is it?" and then work day and night to become an 'expert'.

In the course of one of my marathon study sessions, I happened across a book called *Wishcraft* by Barbara Sher. That book literally changed my life! Years later, when I was a workshop presenter at NATCON, the National Consultation on Career Development, Barbara Sher was the keynote speaker and, because as a speaker I had the exciting privilege of relaxing in the speaker's lounge, I met her and told her that her book had changed my life. Looking back, I just hope I didn't gush and fawn like some star-struck teenager.

In *Wishcraft*, Barbara Sher suggested writing out a description of your ideal day. It was to be extremely detailed, in the first person and in the present tense. I tried it. You'll get to try it too, later in the book. I wrote about three pages describing my perfect life, complete with little house of my own, an SUV and a German shepherd. In my perfect life I would be working for myself doing career counselling and I'd be fulfilled, happy and successful.

It was so much fun doing that first ideal day. I was a daydreamer anyway so this was right up my alley. I did more of them. I did ideal rainy days, ideal snowy days, ideal weekend days, ideal work days. And I read them over and over and refined them.

Then, out of the blue, I was asked to teach a life skills program for people on social assistance. By then welfare was just a bleak memory for me and I think I was seen as someone who could provide not only the information but a role model for the participants. I didn't really know what a life skills program was, so as usual when I suddenly had to be an 'expert', I went to the library and took out every book I could find on the subject. This time my research didn't help and after I showed up the first day with a completely inadequate plan, one of my new colleagues set me straight on what was included in 'life skills'. It was all about helping the clients deal with the challenges of everyday life–communications, problem solving, and goal setting. I learned so much teaching that program and started to develop some practical sessions with real life applications.

As part of the program, just before New Years, I led the group in a full day session where they visualized and then wrote out and shared their ideal day.

Everyone was so uplifted and motivated by the workshop that I made it an annual event for a few years. I felt like I had come home. I loved helping others to see their future and encouraging them to make changes.

At that point it was enjoyable and fulfilling work but I had no real evidence that it was changing people's lives in any significant way. A couple of years went by and I continued working in the field but my fascination with 'ideal days' waned. The little file of 'ideal days' that I had been so faithfully reading was put aside and I didn't create any new ones for a while. My son grew up and moved out and I was ready to make changes in my life. At the end of 1993, I was still living in the housing co-op where I had raised my son but when a friend offered to give me one of his German shepherd puppies I was forced to move. In that housing complex we were only allowed pets with a total of eight legs. Since I already had two cats I was over the leg limit and I had to choose—keep living in a police state situation or move on. I chose to buy a house.

As I was packing for my move, I found all those ideal days I had written and there was my present life, in extreme detail, written out in black and white!

I had the little house with a big fenced yard. I had a Chevy Blazer SUV. I had a German shepherd named Ruby. I was self employed doing career coaching and leading workshops. It was the life of my 'ideal days'. The ideal day exercise had actually worked!

That day I began to understand the power of our dreams, the power of our thoughts. It was long before *The Secret* and it was considered pretty off-the-wall, so I didn't really use it often in my career coaching or workshops unless I felt the people were open to the ideas I had. Occasionally I had a client that I could talk to about exciting new concepts like living an authentic life and visualization. That gave me the chance to explore new tools and exercises to help clients and workshop participants start changing their lives. From these people I collected stories that reinforced what I now knew to be true—that we have an amazing power to shape our reality and create the lives we dream of.

I had always daydreamed of becoming a writer. That's what started this whole journey really. Now the daydream had coalesced into an intention to write a book that would pull together all that I had learned about how to cultivate and use our innate power as co-creators of our lives.

This book is my dream come true. It is the result of over twenty-five years of studying, experimenting and trying to live the life I was meant to live. It includes many of the tools and exercises that I've seen work for clients and that I'm sure will work for you.

Down the road, not too far in the future, when you are living your dream, living the life you were born to live, I hope you will contact me and tell me your story.

I look forward to it.

Is This the Life You Were Born to Live?

There are only two ways to live your life. One is as though nothing is a miracle. The other is as though everything is a miracle.
                                            -Albert Einstein

Do you sometimes feel like something is missing in your life? Not sure what exactly, but something. Passion maybe? Or a compelling reason to get up in the morning? Do you feel like you're wandering through life, lost and not quite finding the road that you should be on? Or do you feel like the road you're on is all uphill, full of rocks, sometimes totally blocked by boulders that force you into a detour? Or is it a superhighway, with no scenery, just a long unbroken yellow line passing you by? Nowhere to get off, rest and enjoy the view? Or maybe you're just in a traffic jam, stalled, not going anywhere?

That's not what your life journey is meant to be. Your life journey should be one of exploration, adventure, joy and fulfillment. It should be like taking an exhilerating hike through a beautiful forest, or along a beach with the ocean roaring beside you, or over hills and into valleys with vistas of grass and flowers and white-topped mountains in the distance. I can't tell you what exactly your journey is meant to be. Only you know that. But I do know your journey should be one that, when it's over, you can say with gusto, "Wow! What a great trip!"

The life path you follow here on this small blue planet should be the one that you were born to travel. Down deep inside you, in the quiet place where your soul lives, you know what that path is and where it should take you. You can connect with that quiet place, your authentic self, the self you were born to be. When you connect, you'll know how your life journey should unfold and if you listen, and follow, you will find that passion and reason to get up every morning.

You won't even have to work at it. You'll be pulled effortlessly, guided by your soul's quiet voice. I call that voice Future Pull and following its call will change your life.

This book is meant to help you connect with your deepest self so that you can clearly envision the life you were meant to live, move into alignment with it, and experience joy and fulfillment in each day. It contains tools and exercises that will make you think, challenge you and ask you to take action. I suggest that you work through it with the help of a group of like-minded individuals. Sometimes it takes others to hold the lantern while you seek the way.

Enjoy the trip!

Make the Connection

Let your mind start a journey thru a strange new world. Leave all thoughts of the world you knew before. Let your soul take you where you long to be. Close your eyes, let your spirit start to soar, and you'll live as you've never lived before.

-Erich Fromm

Make the Connection

Things do not change, we change.
-Henry David Thoreau

I wish I could just give you a few instructions, perhaps a checklist, and say, "do this and this and this," and your ideal life would suddenly materialize. Unfortunately, I've found that, without some preparation, you'd end up going through the motions and then you'd give up and write it off as just another scam.

I've found that when it comes to change, and we are talking about creating massive change in your life here, there are several doorways that you can enter. You can just change your behaviour and some change will result. If you want to lose weight, change your eating habits and you'll lose weight. But if you keep thinking the same thoughts that led to overeating in the first place, you'll gain all that weight back. If you are deeply in debt, you can arrange for someone to administer your funds ruthlessly until all your bills are paid and you're debt-free. But if you haven't changed your way of relating to money, the collectors will be calling you again within a year.

If you want to create lasting change, you have to change your mind before you change your behaviour. If you want to work with the Universe to create the life of your dreams, you must make the connection between how you think and feel and how your life unfolds. You have to plug into the energy of the Universe, but you can't do that if you aren't clear on what that is or how to make the connection.

We are talking about potentially changing every aspect of your life, so adjusting your thinking is not an option—it's a requirement. I'm asking you to change the way you view reality, your place in the Universe, and the level of power you have in creating your life. It's mind-bending!

In this section, you'll be wrapping your mind around several new ideas. Some may be familiar to you; some may be brand new and even frightening. Read on with an open mind!

Adopt a Perspective of Unlimited Possibility

> *Limitations live only in our minds. But if we use our imaginations, our possibilities become limitless.*
> -Jamie Paolinetti

    I am asking you to open your mind to the possibilities, to consider that perhaps things that seem impossible now, may be possible, and that we just don't know how or why—YET.

    I am going to share an embarrassing secret. Don't spread it around. It's this—if there is more than one way to interpret something, I will always, inevitably, choose the wrong way. For example, the year after Hurricane Katrina devastated New Orleans, there was another hurricane heading directly for the city. I was watching CNN as the city prepared for the hurricane's landfall and heard the mayor of New Orleans make strong statements about the consequences of anyone taking advantage of the situation by looting. He said something like, "There will be zero tolerance for looting. Any looters will be sent directly to Angola." I was shocked. I thought, "Whoa! How can they do that? Wouldn't the government of Angola have something to say about that? Maybe Angola doesn't want all of America's criminals! What is Angola, some kind of planetary prison state? That's ridiculous!" I worked myself into quite a flurry, but a few minutes later I found out that Angola is the Louisiana State Penitentiary. I felt a little silly but I couldn't help but chuckle.

Another time, I read the headline, "Crack found in lining of shuttle." Immediately, again jumping to another completely off-base conclusion, I thought,

"Wow! You'd think astronauts would be a better quality of person. I'm surprised that crack addicts would pass all that screening." Of course, reading the actual article revealed that it was a structural problem in the shuttle and that astronauts are not just a bunch of crack heads wanting to experience a new high in space. I had a really good chuckle after that one.

Remember when Dolly the sheep was cloned in 1996? It was the first time a mammal had been cloned and made headlines around the world. When I read it, I thought I was misinterpreting as usual. Now I admit that I was completely behind the times, but I didn't have any idea that cloning was anywhere near reality. I thought it was still strictly in the science fiction realm.

Finding out that they had successfully cloned an animal was a major turning point for me. First of all, I now try to stay a little more informed so that I don't sound as stupid as I did when Dolly happened. I'm also much more open-minded about what is possible. Other people have 'ah-hah moments'. I have 'Dolly moments'. A

Dolly moment is when my mind's door creaks open just a little wider.

Since my first Dolly moment, I have adopted a Perspective of Unlimited Possibility. Now I think that, until it's proven that something is impossible, who can say whether it is or isn't. I try to balance that with the realization that it's dangerous to be too gullible. You know the old saying about what happens when you're too open-minded–your brains might fall out.

Although my formal education in math and science was limited to business math in grades nine and ten, I have become a voracious reader of anything related to physics. One thing that becomes obvious the more you read about the new lines of exploration and discovery in science, particularly quantum physics, is that even the experts, the scientists working every day to decode and explain the nature of reality and consciousness, are finding that the more they know, the more they don't know.

It appears that as we step into the future, we are learning that perhaps some of the ancient beliefs about energy and reality have more substance than we previously thought. Of course, I'm not suggesting that we go back to believing ancient myths where thunder and rain and the rising and setting of the sun were powered up by gods and goddesses who were either angry or pleased with the actions of the humans here on earth. Those interpretations of natural phenomena were simplistic and egocentric attempts to explain the then unexplainable. However, I am suggesting that the core beliefs behind many of the myths are perhaps not so far off the mark as we've thought.

It's only very recently that the body-mind connection has become accepted in mainstream society. It's not unusual now for someone to believe that how you think might affect how you feel. We know that stress, which is largely affected by our perception of reality and how we feel about what is actually happening, sets off a myriad of physical responses in the body, and if not mitigated or controlled, is a leading cause of illness and death. This is widely accepted but in the early 1990s when I was teaching stress management courses at the local college, it was leading edge information. We also know that if someone changes their thinking, perhaps their perception of themselves and their ability to influence and control their physical bodies, they can effect truly amazing miracles of healing.

Compare today's understanding of the mind-body connection with the ancient beliefs about shamans and medicine men and their powers. Voodoo dolls may be the stuff of horror movies but their real life effect is just as strong as anything you might see in the movies. In an Australian tribal culture, they used a stick instead of a voodoo doll. If you were angry with someone or felt they had done you wrong, you could go to the shaman or, in this case, the witch doctor, and for a fee he would point a stick at the offending person. Within days the victim of the stick would begin to sicken and die. In fact, 'pointing the stick' was outlawed and punishable by imprisonment in that country. Perhaps that's not so different from the damage that we know stress can cause. Death by voodoo doll or death by pink slip?

Ultimately, it's still death as a result of our own thinking.

And what about the placebo effect? Numerous studies have demonstrated that if you give someone a sugar pill and tell them that it is medicine that has an 80% to 90% success rate in curing whatever ails them, there is a very good chance that they will indeed get better. Or the power of visualization to cure illness? Patients with terminal illnesses who put their disease into remission by visualizing the tumour being dissolved or gobbled up by a video game character? Is that any different than people who have been cured by the rattles and chanting of a shaman? They are examples of ideas that were laughed at and ridiculed as being the beliefs of primitive people and now have been proven to have a scientific basis.

Now I'm asking you to adopt a Perspective of Unlimited Possibility and to consider that you might have far more power over reality than these few examples demonstrated. I'm suggesting that you have the power to co-create your life and manifest your deepest desires. As you listen or read about new ideas and possibilities, instead of immediately dismissing them and thinking them too farfetched to be real, just consider that there is the possibility that you just may not know everything there is to know and that anything is possible. Be a child again with a willingness to believe.

There are certain beliefs or views of reality that, once assumed to be true, have the power to immediately and amazingly affect the direction and quality of your life. A Perspective of Unlimited Possibility is a way of viewing reality that will lead to an amazing change in your life. Does that statement sound too extravagant–that a change in perspective can affect the direction and quality of your life? Amazing means that you will view the results with awe and wonder. I am absolutely confident that if you accept, or at least try this on for size, you will be amazed at the results. If you adopt the Perspective of Unlimited Possibility and apply it on a continuous basis, you will create positive and massive change in your life. Guaranteed!

So what is a Perspective of Unlimited Possibility? By adopting a Perspective of Unlimited Possibility, I have chosen to take an open-minded approach to the array of possibilities that each new scientific discovery opens up. I have shed the safe haven of dogmatic belief and I am willing to venture forth to explore all that life has to offer. In the middle ages, maps of the known world had drawings of sea monsters beyond the edges of the land. Only the bravest sailors would venture out of sight of land in case 'there be monsters' or in case they fell off the edge of the earth.

Helen Keller's words, "Life is either a daring adventure or nothing" is my motto. I think of myself as one of those brave sailors willing to view life as a grand adventure to be undertaken. I want to open my eyes and my mind and my heart to all the possibilities in life. I am willing to take the chance that I might meet monsters because I know they are all just in my mind anyway. I know that it's not likely that I'll fall off the edge of the earth and much more likely that I'll discover wonderful new lands and fantastic new experiences.

When I adopt a Perspective of Unlimited Possibility, I see a myriad of possibilities in life and am willing to explore them. You can be an adventurer too. Just adopt the Perspective of Unlimited Possibility.

The Nature of Time

If I look confused, it's because I'm thinking.
                                    -Samuel Goldwyn

It's a beautiful sunny Sunday morning. We had flurries overnight and the roads are all covered with relatively untrammeled snow. I wonder how long it will be before the plow comes.

That brief paragraph has at least four references to time. I mention a day of the week. Ever wonder why we have seven days in a week? Why not five? Or ten? Was it always that way? What is always? I tell you that it's morning. Who decided when morning becomes afternoon and afternoon becomes evening? The establishment of world time zones and Daylight Saving Time means we no longer determine that it is noon when the sun is highest in the sky. Instead, a clock tells us that it is noon.

I mentioned that there was snow overnight and wondered how long it would be before the plows came. How long is long? How do we measure how long and who decided that? And does everyone agree? Is that just my interpretation of time passing? What do I mean by time passing? How does it move and where is it going?

Have I blown your mind yet? A Sunday morning seems as good a time (there I go again, referring to time) as any to ponder the imponderables. It's almost as if you can hardly form a thought without time being woven into it somehow. It appears that time is an integral part of our awareness of being human and being alive.

Perhaps you haven't given the topic of time a great deal of deep thought. After all, we begin to accept the concept of time at a very young age, about the same time that we develop memory and language, and we buy into whatever is the prevailing belief; which, by the way, is not as universal and as long-standing as you might think.

It wasn't until 1884 that nations agreed to standardize time. It wasn't until 1967 that a precise definition for a second was determined. Before that it was considered to be 1/86,400th of a solar day. Problem is, the length of a day varies in length, so by extension the length of a second varies as well. Now, a second is defined as 'the duration of 9,192,631,770 vibrations' of a particular isotope of cesium. And if that isn't enough precision for you, did you know that the earth is slowing down and that as a result, 'leap seconds' need to be inserted to keep the earth's rotation in sync with atomic time. Without this adjustment, in a few thousand years, noon will arrive in the middle of the night. The 'leap second' system isn't perfect but the international organization responsible for deciding how we count time has delayed the decision. They said, "More time is required to build consensus."

I will take a more philosophical approach to this discussion of the nature of time. Jeff Goldsmith, a well-known spiritual teacher, called life "A Parenthesis in Eternity". This imagery is similar to that in this quote by philosopher Philip Novak, "One plunges into time's terrible surf, only to emerge riding its wake, awakened." They both suggest that time is only a function of being here, being alive, and that before and after our human experience we are part of the eternal and timeless. Hold on a second. Who says there is anything that is eternal and timeless? Science is still arguing that. Did time begin with the big bang? If it did, what came before?

I'd like to prepare your mind, like the soil in a garden, to consider some mind-blowing ideas related to the nature of time. A little digging up of long held beliefs, some turning over of accepted concepts, a handful of idea fertilizer and you will be ready to adopt a Perspective of Unlimited Possibility with regard to time and how it works. I'd like you to consider, if you were given the power and the authority to reinvent time, how would you do it?

To reinvent time, you will find it necessary to consider these questions, among many others: What is time? Is it a thing? A feeling? Is it a wave? Or just an illusion of the collective unconscious? Perhaps it's a mass hallucination. Or maybe it's an agreement that we buy into when choosing to become human for this short (define short) visit to earth.

How does time travel? Does time travel? Is time travel possible? And if it is, can we go back and change history? Can we jump forward or just travel through a wormhole to the past?

Does time flow from past to future or from future to past and off into history? What is history? Is history gone or is it still out there somewhere in a parallel universe? Or perhaps time doesn't move at all and we are the ones passing by as though we are riding a moving sidewalk at the airport. Or maybe time is just a series of 'nows', like each of the frames in an old movie reel.

Are you going to make time dependent on the movement of the earth, sun, stars? Or are you going to make it independent of the rest of the universe? Will you adjust the length of the pieces of time? The hours, weeks, months, years? Are you going to make it a little more organized so that we don't have to throw in leap years, or leap seconds, to get things back on track every four years? Are you going to announce that all months are now thirty days, or thirty-one or twenty-five so that we don't have to remember that silly little rhyme—thirty days hath September....?

Is the past etched in stone? Is the future just a mirage? Or is the future pre-determined? Is the past just a poorly remembered work of fiction? Do we 'remember' the future or imagine it?

Go get a coffee, sit down, relax and consider the nature of time. But perhaps you should set an alarm because when you start to rethink time, you'll be heading off down a rabbit hole and you may forget to come out. And by the way, is forgetting a function of time passing? And is time different when you're down the rabbit hole or in another dimension?

If you are starting to think that I'm being ridiculous and that surely science has the answers to these questions, think again. These are not just the meanderings of a mind that is woefully under-informed about physics, whether that be classical mechanical theory or quantum theory; these are the questions that 'real' physicists are exploring. They are also arguing about the answers and certainly nowhere close to agreement.

Let me provide a simple, as simple as I can given the subject, overview of some of the key ideas that are relevant to the concept of Future Pull and the suggestion that you can create your future and flow into it.

If we don't think too deeply about it, time seems simple enough. After all, it surrounds us, governs our lives and is the foundation of conscious human experience. It appears to be so integral to our experience that it seems to be internally controlled as though time begins with our first breath and ends with our last.

The metaphors we use for time reinforce the common view, at least the common Western view, that time flows in a straight line from the past, through the now, and on into the future. We refer to it as a 'river' or an 'arrow'. We talk of 'looking back' at the past or 'looking ahead' to the future. Time appears to flow in one direction only. We view it as a limited commodity and speak of 'wasting time', 'saving time', 'using time wisely' and 'managing time'. We say it crawls or flies by depending on whether we are having an enjoyable time or suffering through it. We can't touch it, smell it or taste it but we think we can feel it. Or at least we think we can feel it passing and we see the wake it leaves as we age.

There are many variations on the 'what is time' theme. St. Augustine of Hippo (AD 354-430) pondered time and came to believe that perhaps it is all just in our heads. If he was right, it's a mass hallucination; a complex agreement with rules and, well, timelines. You may want to brush off St. Augustine's conclusion as a 'dark ages' idea like 'the world is flat'. Far from it. Some present day physicists also believe that time may be an illusion. Even one of the greatest thinkers of all time considered that perhaps time is illusory. Einstein thought that perhaps time is not 'out there' but 'in here'; an internal perception or feeling that time is passing.

Another way of viewing time is as part of a space-time block in which past and future have equal status and that 'now' is just a label like 'here'. That might mean that time is real but that its flow is an illusion. It may be hard to wrap your mind around that idea. After all, evidence of the passing of time is all around us. We see fossils embedded in rock that tell us that millions of years have passed since those creatures lived. Looking up at the stars at night, knowing how fast light travels and calculating how many light years away they are, we conclude that the light from them has been on course to us for millions of years. Astronomers' best guess is that 14 billion years have passed since the birth of the Universe. So if time isn't passing, what is it doing?

Einstein's special theory of relativity opened the door to the space-time concept and the idea that time is actually a fourth dimension. You can go to YouTube to view animations of four dimensional objects but be warned, in this case seeing doesn't necessarily mean understanding. Some physicists view space-time as evidence that past, present and future could all be here with us now, similar to the block universe idea.

A commonly held perspective is that the future is a mirage while the past is etched in stone. But is it? It appears that our memories are fragile and not particularly trustworthy. If that is the case, is the past any more sure than the future? Quantum mechanics tells us that the future is one of 'potential' and 'possibility'. The 'now' may be all that is real or 'for sure'. 'Presentism' suggests that both the past and the future can be considered part of the 'now'. Our memory of the past is based in 'now' and the future is as we imagine it 'now'. The present contains our memories of the past as well as our expectations of the future.

Quantum mechanics is all about possibility and probability. It tells us that a particle cannot be definitely placed or located until it is actually measured. Until it is measured in time and space it is only a probability with an infinite number of possibilities. To add to the confusion for us poor amateurs, there is the even more complicated 'quantum entanglement' or 'quantum non-locality'. This means that two entangled particles, each one of a pair of connected particles, can communicate even at great distances. Conceivably, because of the space-time fabric of reality, each of them could be, simultaneously, at a different point in time, not only at a different point in space. Therefore, because they are entangled and communicating, they would be both here right now and here in the future, at the same time.

This is time travel at the micro-level, but it gives rise to and adds credibility to the possibility of time travel at the macro-level. Travelling to the future, albeit just tiny tiny distances into the future, is already possible due to space travel. Astronauts travel forward in time, although the amount of time forward that they move is minuscule. Travelling backward is seen as potentially possible but gives rise to troubling paradoxes.

Time travel requires that there be a 'past' or 'future' to travel to. Is there a 'past' sitting back there somewhere waiting to be visited? Is there a 'future' already existing up ahead? The parallel universe theory has been around since the mid 1950s and, in a nutshell, suggests that every time there is an event with more than one possible outcome, all the outcomes occur, each in a separate universe. The parallel universes idea is something like the 'choose your own adventure' children's books that were popular in the 1980s. All the possible endings were contained in the book and, at critical points, you would make a decision as to the action to be taken by the hero and then follow the story as it unfolded based on that decision.

Mental time travel is a term used to describe travelling to the past or future via our memory or imagination. It was first used by Canadian neuroscientist Endel Tulving. He said, "Remembering, for the rememberer, is mental time travel; a sort of reliving of something that happened in the past."

Modern neuroscience suggests that remembering the past is very similar to imagining the future. Both use similar parts of the brain's frontal and temporal lobes. It appears that remembering the more distant past is more difficult than recent events. Similarly, envisioning the distant future is harder than imagining the near future. Moreover, as we age, our ability to remember the past or 'see' the future shrinks from both ends. I can't help but wonder if we find it harder to see a far off future because it isn't there. Perhaps we can only see into the future as far as our personal future goes.

Which leads me to the nature of time and Future Pull. We now know that time is certainly not a clearly defined, mapped out, agreed upon concept. Far from it. We see that the more we know, the more we don't know. Every discovery creates more questions than it answers. Pondering time and how it flows requires us to adopt a Perspective of Unlimited Possibilities.

So here's a thought: What if our future is already up there waiting for us? I'm not talking about fate, although the implication that we have the power to pre-determine our future is perhaps on target. If we are self-determining, and I believe we are, we live our lives; our lives don't live us. But what if we can create, ahead of time, with the power of our imagination and visualization, a future life that we can flow into?

What if we can create such a compelling vision of our future as we want it to be, that we actually create it, up there ahead of us? What if we could create a future so clear and so powerful that it pulled us toward it effortlessly? That is the concept of Future Pull.

Future Pull

Today you are You, that is truer than true. There is no one alive that is Youer than You.
                                        -Dr. Seuss

I want to take you back to a time long ago and maybe far away. Back to the moment in time when your mother and your father came together in a moment of primal intimacy and two bundles of cells containing completely different DNA collided and became one. The unique bundle of cells that was created in that moment contained the blueprint for the person you are now.

Do you have any idea how unique you are? Ryan J. Sokol of Texas A&M

University calculated the odds of someone EXACTLY like you being born. First he estimated the total number of fertile men and women in the world, calculated the number of different genetic possibilities a man might contribute, adjusted for the number of hours of female fertility each month and then factored in a long list of other considerations. After all that math, far far too complicated for me to understand, he stated that, "The chance that you, meaning exactly you, would ever be born are 1 in 1.3 times ten to the twenty-ninth power." So in not much simpler terms, the odds of another you being born are 130,000,000,000,000,000,000,000,000,000 to one. To put that in perspective, according to a CBC News report on November 9, 2009, your chances of being killed by lightning are 1 in 56,439 and your chances of winning over $15 million in the lottery are about 1 in 28,633,528. You are so lucky to be alive and so lucky to be you!

No one like you has ever existed before and no one like you will ever exist again, or at least the likelihood of that is so remote as to be considered impossible.

Add to that the influence of environment. Even twins, who are more alike than two strangers or even two fraternal siblings, still continue to develop their own uniqueness as they grow and develop and interact with the world and people around them. Though you might have grown up in a household with the same parents, going to the same school, you and your brother or sister see every single event from a different perspective, react to it in a different way and change as a result of that event to a different degree. It boggles the mind!

Your purpose in undertaking this amazing adventure on earth and the life path you were born to follow is just as unique as you are. However, from the moment of your birth, you are conditioned to fit into a certain mould. You quickly learn what is acceptable and what isn't. You soon forget how unique you are and that you came here to experience your own adventure. You are trained to 'fit in' and be like everyone else.

To some extent this works well for us. We learn social skills so that we can interact with others, make friends, get what we want and need to thrive, and become a contributing member of our chosen society. We learn the language of our 'tribe', table manners, how to use money. We learn the history of our culture so that we have a reference point for our place in time and space. All of this conditioning is crucial to our ability to function effectively in society.

But it comes with a price. We lose some of our individuality and we lose our way. That's when we begin to wander instead of following our life path. That's when we start to wonder who we are and what we should be doing. We feel lost and empty because we've lost the connection to our deepest self—the self who chose to come here and embark on this great and wondrous journey. We feel a yearning for 'more'.

That yearning is Future Pull. It's your deepest self calling out to be let free. Don't worry, it doesn't mean you have to sell all your belongings and head off into the wilderness to live alone—well, not unless that's what you really want to do. Surprisingly, you'll probably find that you've had some clues as to where you should be heading and you may have already taken some steps in that direction. Your dreams and wishes are like little gold nuggets that wash up on the bank of a stream. They are just clues to the rich gold vein that lies so close.

Originally the term Future Pull was coined to describe a strategic planning process for businesses. A team would create a compelling vision for the future of the company so that everyone would align with it and be inspired to achieve it. It was a first step in developing organizational goals and objectives.

Future Pull can also be compared to the way the DNA in all living things acts as a blueprint for the organism. When an apple seed grows, it becomes an apple tree – not a maple tree or an oak tree. When a robin's egg hatches, an eagle doesn't struggle out. A cat won't give birth to a rabbit. The entire apple tree, robin or cat is contained in the collection of living cells that transforms into a full-grown tree, bird or animal. Just as they should. It's one of the laws of the Universe. Of course, just as with us, environment plays a part too. The apple tree will only grow to its full potential if it has the right conditions – good soil, sun, water.

The difference between that tree and you is that, as a human, you have free will and the ability to exercise it. The tree can't pull up its roots and head for sunnier ground. But you can. You are self-determining and have the ability to choose your direction in life and seek out what you need to become your very best self.

There is another way to describe Future Pull and this is the meaning proposed in this book. This view of Future Pull challenges us to take a Perspective of Unlimited Possibility in our view of time. As we discussed previously, most people think of time as a line that extends from the past–way back there–to the future– way up ahead. They see it as a smooth, unbroken, straight line with a little point labelled 'now'. What if time is not a constant, unbroken, arrow? What if it circles round and bends back on itself? What if there are different realities and dimensions and 'right now' is happening in all of them? We've seen that science is exploring the nature of time and that what they are finding creates more questions than it answers.

As I have suggested, we are self-determining and live our lives–our lives don't live us. But just maybe, the flow of time is such that the future is up there already ahead of us and we have the power, with our minds, to create the life that we move into. Perhaps we can create a future so clear and so powerful that it pulls us toward it effortlessly.

The idea of creating your own reality is not a new one. After all, we know that if, for example, someone you accept as knowledgable and credible tells you that you have an 80% chance of getting ill or dying, there's a good chance that you will, in fact, get ill or die. If you believe that something will happen and you focus on it, there's a pretty good chance that what you think will happen, will in fact come to pass. We call that a self-fulfilling prophecy. We usually see that in a negative context. But it doesn't have to be a negative self-fulfilling prophecy. You can predict a positive experience and have that come to pass too.

That is what Future Pull is all about. Future Pull is when you envision your future with such clarity and power that it literally pulls you towards it. Things fall into place, synchronicity happens, opportunities arise, and you move closer and closer to your vision of the future–without pain and struggle. Sound miraculous?

Miracles happen every day. They are only miracles because we don't yet have an explanation. Keep your mind open to the possibilities. Adopt a Perspective of Unlimited Possibility.

The Law of Attraction

We are what we think...
All that we are,
arises with our thoughts.
With our thoughts
we make our world.
                    -Buddha

There are some concepts that make sense or have been proven scientifically, and I accept them as fact. There are some ideas that are interesting and I'm willing to consider them as possibilities. As Carl Sagan said, "Somewhere, something incredible is waiting to be known." Then there are the things that I believe with my whole heart–in spite of not having proof or knowing how exactly they work. Call it an intuitive 'knowing' if you will. That is when I adopt the Perspective of Unlimited Possibility. I open my mind and allow the possibility that certain unproven things might be true.

In the Bible, Paul wrote, in Hebrews 11:1, "Faith is the assured expectation of things hoped for, the evident demonstration of realities though not beheld." Sometimes we may absolutely believe that something is true in spite of not understanding the why's and how's of it.

Let me use a simple analogy. If I flick the switch on the wall in my kitchen the light comes on and I can see. I don't know how it works but I know that if I've paid my hydro bill, it usually happens just as I expect. If I knew more about the why's and how's of it, I'd be able to change that fixture for something more attractive without calling an electrician. But in my day to day world, the evident demonstration of reality is that electricity flows through my walls, through wires, and lights up my kitchen.

Thich Nhat Hanh was a Vietnamese Buddhist monk, author, poet, and peace activist. He was a leader in 'engaged Buddhism' which melded traditional Zen Buddhism with ideas from Western psychology and the pursuit of change and human freedoms. He was nominated for a Nobel Peace Prize by Martin Luther King Jr., but his stance against the Vietnam War led to his exile to France in 1973. He wrote,

> "In April, we cannot see sunflowers in France, so we might say the sunflowers do not exist. But the local farmers have already planted thousands of seeds, and when they look at the bare hills, they may be able to see the sunflowers already. The sunflowers are there. They lack only the conditions of sun, heat, rain and July. Just because we cannot see them does not mean that they do not exist."

One of the concepts that I have faith in and live my life by is what is now called the Law of Attraction. I've seen "the evident demonstration of realities though not beheld" both in my own life and in the lives of others.

Have you heard of the Law of Attraction? Most likely you have. Although the actual concept has been around for centuries, it was in the late nineteenth century that the New Thought Movement began to spread the idea that our brains can influence our environment. The name, "The Law of Attraction" wasn't actually coined until it appeared in the works of William Walker Atkinson, writing under one of his many pseudonyms, Theron Q. Dumont. In 1906, he wrote *Thought Vibration or the Law of Attraction in the Thought World*. Other writers, including the prolific Emmet Fox, author of *The Seven Day Mental Diet*, and Napoleon Hill, who wrote one of the best-selling books of all time, *Think and Grow Rich*, went on to suggest techniques and tools to help people use their thinking to change their lives. But the Law of Attraction was delegated to the 'woo-woo' file by most people until the movie, *The Secret*, was released in 2006.

Now the Law of Attraction has gone mainstream and people around the world are choosing sides. Is the Law of Attraction for real? Is the Law of Attraction the most important and powerful law of the Universe? Or is it just more evidence of the gullibility of people looking for a quick fix to their problems? I'm assuming that since you've gotten this far in this book, you are at least leaning toward the idea that there might be some merit to the idea of the Law of Attraction.

Perhaps you have even tried it for yourself — created a vision board, visualized, recited daily affirmations in front of the mirror — and maybe your results were mixed. Now you're looking for the real 'secret', that missing ingredient that will make the difference between so-so results and really manifesting the life you were meant to live.

Well I have good news and bad news. It's not a big secret. The good news is that the Law of Attraction is for real and it really can change your life. The bad news is that it isn't quite as simple as the film made it appear. You can't just place an order with the Universe via your vision board and then wait for all the goodies to show up. It requires more than that – a change of mind, patience, trust, and yes, even some work.

The Secret did a great service for us all by making the Law of Attraction mainstream. It opened millions of people's minds to the possibility that they actually can work with the universe to manifest their deepest desires. But it was a movie and it was simplified to make it palatable. Another movie, *What the Bleep Do We Know*, released in 2004, covered the topic in far more detail. Its extended version, *Down the Rabbit Hole*, explored it even further and included interviews that explained some of the science behind the Law of Attraction.

Don't get me wrong! The Law of Attraction will work no matter what you do. In fact, it is working—24/7—whether you believe it or not. Whether you dismiss it as hooey or faithfully spend twenty minutes every day visualizing a new relationship entering your life, the Law of Attraction is affecting your life all day every day.

It's very simple really. The Law of Attraction means that whatever things, people, events, opportunities and situations you think about, focus on and feel strongly about, you will attract into your life.

I bet you think you are doing that right? After all, what about those twenty minutes of visualizing the man of your dreams knocking on your door joyfully proclaiming, "I'm here?" If you are spending the rest of your day thinking about how lonely you are and feeling jealous of your happily married friends, you are going to continue to see singleness and loneliness showing up in your life. You see, the feeling part of the equation is the most powerful part of the equation. So if you try to think one way but feel another way, the attraction power of the way you feel will trump the attraction power of your thoughts.

I know, I've done it all wrong too. In fact, I still have to be careful. It's so easy to drop your vigilance and let negative thoughts or worrying thoughts take over.

For example, recently I was talking with a friend about falling. I had fallen a few weeks before and I had a small injury in my shoulder as a result. I was joking about how klutzy I've always been and we compared falling stories. I mentioned that I do worry about falling since I've had two knee replacements and I expect that it will really hurt if I fall on them. The very next day, as I was stepping up onto a curb, it suddenly became two feet high and I tripped over it. Okay, perhaps it didn't physically grow two feet but it sure seemed like it. I flew out, sprawling face first, right there in public. Luckily, I didn't land on my knees but I couldn't help but remember how focused I've been on not 'falling', worrying about it and talking about it. Falling being the key word here. So of course I fell. And I know better than that.

A long time ago I wanted to lose some weight, so I bought a poster of a very obese naked woman sitting surrounded by a feast of food and stuffing it into her open mouth. I hung it on the fridge so that every time I was tempted to eat, I'd see it and be repulsed and refrain from eating. Of course, I took it down when I was expecting visitors because it really was a horrendous looking thing. Guess what happened? I continued to eat and I gained weight.

Even a new student of the Law of Attraction can see where I was going wrong. I was focusing on my weight and eating rather than on my real goal, which was to be fit and healthy and slim.

Here's another example that might ring a bell for you. You want to get out of debt. You decide that you want to win a million dollars in the lottery. That will definitely get you out of debt. Every day you close your eyes and recite, "I am getting out of debt" exactly twenty-one times. Yes, I learned that at a seminar. According to that expert, reciting your affirmation exactly twenty-one times is the key. The problem is, that is a bad affirmation. You want your debt to diminish – key word 'debt'. You wait for some unexpected windfall. You start to doubt and wonder why the Universe isn't coming through for you. And after a week of affirmations, you wake up late one morning and rush off to work without doing your daily twenty-one and that is the end of that. Sound familiar?

The Law of Attraction does really work. It's not even hard or complicated. But you do have to understand how it works and work with it. That's a key piece. The Law of Attraction is really about co-creating your life with the Universe. It's not all up to the Universe. You can't just decide what you want and then send an order out to the Universe and wait for it to show up at your door like a parcel from UPS, the Universal Postal Service. You are a partner with the Universe and you have to do your share of the co-creating. You have to actually take some action and do some work on your end too.

Then there's another key part of the equation that is often forgotten—Allowing. You have to be home when the parcel from the Universe shows up. You don't know how and when the Universe is going to come through on its end and you have to be patient, trusting, and persistent and learn how to recognize and accept the Universe's help.

Allowing is the part of the Law of Attraction that I used to have the most trouble remembering and applying. I am what a friend has called an 'over-eee-er'. When I start to think that things are going sideways and I forget that things always work out as they should, I start to 'eeeeee'. I go, "Eeeee, why didn't I get that job?" "Eeeee, what's that noise in my car engine?" "Eeeeee, what if it rains tomorrow when I have my deck party planned." What a waste of worry and energy!

And then of course, later when things do work out as they should, I look back and think, "Darn, I did it again!" I wasted so much time and energy worrying about things when I should know by now that it all works out for the best in the end. I have learned that if you relax and trust, stay focused on what you want to happen–the big picture rather than the small details–it really does work out in the end.

Our Universe is not one of uncontrolled chaos. There is an underlying orderliness and purpose and it applies not only to the great big Universe but even to each of us individuals. We are never subject to luck or the whims of fate. There is a reason and a purpose for every turn in our lives. We just may not necessarily know what that reason or purpose is when we are experiencing it. Often it is revealed to us later, when we can appreciate it. But it takes trust to allow it all to unfold as it should.

A few years ago, I presented that point of view in a workshop. One man commented, "Isn't that just positive thinking; looking for the best in things?" I could tell by the way he said 'positive thinking' that he didn't necessarily see that as being very positive. I asked him, "What kind of thinking would you recommend, if not positive thinking?" He stated, firmly, "Realistic thinking." However, whether you choose negative or positive thoughts, what you are thinking is going to turn up as your reality. If you choose negative thinking, you will end up with negative reality. If you choose positive thinking, you will find positive reality showing up. So, since I have a choice, I choose the positive.

I choose to believe, when things are difficult and I start to wonder why, that there is a reason and a season for everything and that if I trust and relax, that things really will work out for the best. And that eventually, down the road, I'll understand why. Does this sound like I'm looking at the world through rose-coloured glasses? Perhaps I am. But like I said, I prefer that to the alternative. I like Susan Bissonette's words, "An optimist is the human personification of spring."

There is a Zen koan that I think is the perfect example of the wisdom of trusting and allowing the Universe to unwind as it should.

"A man lived in a small mountain village. He had a son that he loved more than life itself. He also had a horse. He was proud of the horse and loved it and cared for it. But one day the horse ran away.

As the man sat on his stool outside of his hut, the neighbours came by and said, "How sad that your horse ran away." And he replied, "Maybe."

Then his son went out looking for the horse and he found it. It had teamed up with a beautiful stallion and they were out galloping over the mountains and enjoying their freedom. The son captured the horse and the stallion and brought them both home.

As the man sat on his stool outside of his hut, the neighbours came by and said, "How wonderful that you have this beautiful new stallion and your horse. You are a very fortunate man." And he replied, "Maybe."

Then as his son was trying to train the stallion, he had an accident and fell off the horse and broke his legs very badly so that he was bedridden for quite a long time.

As the man sat on his stool outside of his hut, the neighbours came by and said, "Oh how sad about your son. You must be so upset over the accident. What bad luck." And he replied, "Maybe."

As the man continued to sit on his stool outside his hut, a group of soldiers came by. A war had started and they were coming to draft all the able-bodied young men to go to fight.

Of course, they had to leave the old man's son at home because of his broken leg."

This story perfectly illustrates that we may not always know the big picture. We are limited in our perceptions. We can't foretell the future. Believing that there is a purpose and order to the Universe helps us to remember to go with the flow and wait to see how it will turn out.

I've seen this approach free people to make major decisions without fear. As a career coach for thirty years, I've often worked with people who are paralyzed by indecision over a career choice. What I try to impress on them is that we cannot predict the future. All we can do is make the best decision that we can, based on the information we have right now, and then trust in the flow of the Universe. When you have a Perspective of Unlimited Possibility, you are willing to allow that anything may happen. When you accept that there is order and purpose to the Universe, the fear over making the wrong decision is reduced and you are open to accept all the wonderful adventures that may be just around the corner.

If you've used the power of Future Pull to create a compelling vision of the life you were born to live, have set clear intentions, and are taking inspired action as you travel your life path, then the Universe will take care of the unknowns. You just need to allow.

When it comes to the Law of Attraction you're in the game whether you believe it or not and whether you want to be in it or not. In that case, you might as well learn how to work with the Law of Attraction rather than against it. Perhaps 'work' is a misleading term. Perhaps we should call it 'play'. 'Play' on the same side as the Law of Attraction and you'll be on the winning team.

The Importance of Gratitude

I would maintain that thanks are the highest form of thought; and that gratitude is happiness doubled by wonder.
                                -G.K. Chesterton

    The feeling and emotion you attach to your thoughts about what you want to pull into your life is the most powerful attraction force you have. Gratitude or appreciation is the most powerful of those feelings.

    Abraham is a collection of non-physical realities that speak through Esther Hicks. Esther and her husband,

Jerry Hicks, travel around North America in a big bus leading workshops and turning people on to the wisdom of Abraham and the Law of Attraction. Abraham, Esther and Jerry have produced numerous books and cd's that document these workshops and they are really the go-to source for information about the Law of Attraction. Abraham distinguishes between gratitude and appreciation and says that appreciation is equal to love and is key to attracting your desires into your life. In the book, *Ask and It Is Given*, Abraham says:

> "Every time you appreciate something, every time you praise something, every time you feel good about something, you are telling the Universe: "More of this, please." You need never make another verbal statement of this intent, and if you are mostly in a state of appreciation, all good things will flow to you."

Appreciation or gratitude has a way of turning our thoughts around and completely changing our attitude from misery to joy. When we count our blessings, we have more to count. Even when things seem low, if you try, you will always be able to find something to be thankful for.

I remember when I first gained that understanding. I had had a horrible day at work. I had received notice that I was being laid off and had only two weeks left to work. Then when I got home I found that my dog had taken a pot of leftover borsht out of the sink and carried it to the living room, onto the carpet, where she had spread it around like a feast before consuming it and throwing up. It appeared that she had then tried to hide the mess by covering it with the dirt from a big floor plant that I had by the door. I thought the carpet was ruined forever.

After I cleaned it all up, I went to put the dirty cleaning rags in the washing machine and found that the load of laundry I had put in to wash in the morning was still sitting in a tub of water. My washing machine had broken. So I pulled out all the clothes, wrung them out by hand the best I could and then put them in a laundry basket to take to the laundromat. As I carried them out, through the living room to the front door, all the water poured out through the side of the basket and left a trail of water through the house. After I had a little weep, I went to the laundromat to rewash and dry the laundry. I was really feeling hard done by.

While I sat waiting for my laundry to finish, I pulled out a little piece of paper from my purse and decided to write down all the good things about that day and compare it to all the bad things that had happened.

Unbelievably, the good things on the list outnumbered the bad! They really did! It was a beautiful day. The carpet, surprisingly, hadn't stained. I had a good car that was paid for. I had severance pay coming and I had skills and a good resume and I was sure I'd get another job soon. In fact, I had quite a list of things to be grateful for.

My mood was lifted. I no longer felt like I wanted to go to bed, listen to country music and drink a bottle of cheap wine. I had renewed energy and was ready to move on to the next adventure. That easily and that quickly.

When I conducted interviews with people who are masters at manifesting about their experiences, and asked for their advice about using the Law of Attraction, I spoke to one young British man, Alex Summer, who told me that he sees gratitude as far more than just saying 'thank you'.

Alex, who has become adept at setting goals and achieving his ideal life, believes that you can't turn gratitude on and off. He says that it must evolve from an emotion to an actual spiritual state. He contemplates gratitude during his daily meditation, reviewing his day and acknowledging the blessings and help he has received from others. He knows that he is worthy of what he requests and receives and that he is part of a cycle; in addition to receiving and expressing gratitude, he must also pay it forward and help others. Being part of the divine source of everything, he is part of the flow and must give as well as receive.

We are energetic beings, little cyclones of universal energy. When we feel gratitude the level of our energy rises and we more easily connect with the energy of the Universe. Gratitude literally activates the Law of Attraction, pulling more of what we are grateful for into our lives. Never underestimate the power of being thankful. Make it a daily habit to express gratitude to the Universe as well as to everyone who crosses our path and contributes to our lives in some way. Focus on appreciating all your blessings for a week and watch how it changes your life.

Recognize Your Power

*That's the thing with magic. You've got to know
it's still here, all around us, or it just stays
invisible for you.*
-Charles de Lint

Throughout history, indigenous people have understood that in order to manifest what they desire—whether that be rain for their crops or money in their bank account—they have to connect with the endless ocean of energy that created and continues to feed the Universe. Some belief systems view this universal energy as an individual or many individuals—gods and goddesses—who feel and act much as we do, although in larger and more dramatic ways. The ego-centric view of the universal energy is reflected in the Bible when we read that God created man in his image. Some belief systems see it as an intelligent energy that, with intent and design, created the Universe and has ongoing involvement in what goes on.

It makes no difference whether you refer to the source of Universal energy as God, Jesus, Allah, Buddha, the Divine, the Oneness, Jehovah, Your Higher Power, Shiva, Zeus, or Ralph, when you approach the Universe and ask for help, with the conviction that your request will be answered, help is sent.

Quantum physics has rapidly moved us beyond believing that we are mechanical creatures, responding strictly in a robotic way to stimuli. We've gone from seeing ourselves and all matter in the Universe as solid, to realizing that we are just bundles of energy that hold together a few particles. The energy and the particles that make up YOU are moving –extremely rapidly–flowing in and out of you and changing constantly. The you that you are right now, physically, will not be the you of tomorrow. Some of your atoms and molecules will be the same but even those, by this time next year, will be replaced by new ones. Next month someone else will be hosting the particles that are you today. So what makes you, YOU?

More and more it appears that YOU are not much more than a 'thought', a 'view', a 'consciousness', living in an ever-changing physical body. Perhaps this consciousness is what you've always thought of as your soul. A rather simplistic way of looking at it would be to say that your soul, your greater self, your little part of the Universe, uses your physical body as a vehicle to move around in and affect others and the world.

It's not uncommon to hear the saying, 'we are spiritual beings having a human experience'. I see it this way: I believe that I am a spiritual being who has chosen to create and clothe myself in this human body so that I can have a life experience with all the good and bad that comes with it. This human body I have created and inhabit is mine–for better or worse, to love and cherish, till death do us part –literally. The me that I see when

I look in the mirror is only the smaller part of the greater me that is one with the Universe.

There are many verses in the Bible that reinforce the idea that we are spiritual beings clothed in a physical body. Isaiah 38:12 for example, talks about death as removing a tent or dwelling place. "My dwelling is removed, and is carried away from me as a shepherd's tent: I have rolled up, like a weaver, my life; he will cut me off from the loom." Hebrews 1:12 says, "You will roll them up like a robe; like a garment they will be changed. But you remain the same, and your years will never end," suggesting that we are eternal beings living a physical experience only for a time. So whether your spiritual beliefs are based on the Bible or not, there is evidence to support the concept that we are bundles of everlasting light and energy wearing, for a short time, a body of flesh and blood.

The Universe, my greater self, my spiritual self, is an integral part of me and can't be separated from the physical me, at least not until death makes my physical self irrelevant. Yes, I am one with the Universe, and so are you. So is everything else in the Universe. We are all connected. The Universe is part of me, part of you, part of all of us. The energy of the Universe flows into and out of and all around everything in the Universe. This energy is infinite in its abundance and possibility. It has created all things and continues to feed all things with life energy. The Universe—that unlimited creative energy—is you. Wow! What power!

You are literally a Sorcerer, using the power of the Universe to create the life that you are living here on earth. The first card following the Fool in the Tarot's Major Arcana is the Magician. The Rider-Waite deck depicts the Magician as a man dressed in red robes, holding a wand in his right hand raised to the sky while his left hand points to the ground. The message is that we are conduits of the energy of the Universe, bringing it down and creating magic right here on earth. Notice that the Magician isn't casting spells or mixing potions; magic tricks are not necessary because we have all the power of the Universe at our fingertips.

If the energy of the Universe is all around us and within us, it follows that it shouldn't be difficult to connect with it to use the power that is available. All we need to do is go deep within ourselves to the constant and everlasting part of us– our greater self, our spiritual self. It's as simple as becoming quiet and calm.

Just as with any skill, as you hone your ability to tap into your power, your ability to attract what you desire is increased. When you know what to ask for, how to ask for it, and how to recognize when the Universe answers, you will understand your power and be able to use it on demand and far more effectively. It's really not that difficult. You must believe that you have a power that can be sourced, send a clear message, focus your intention in a strong and positive way, and then remain open and receptive to the reply.

Unfortunately, we often have to dig through a lot of conditioning and mental junk to get to the quiet place where we can connect to our greater self. We have all those limiting beliefs that we've accepted. They shut down our channel of power and communication with our greater self. You may be 'iffy' about whether there really is a source of universal energy. You may doubt that you can access it. You may feel inadequate or undeserving of what you ask for. So often we don't recognize or acknowledge our power or just don't know how to use it. What a shame! So much power at our fingertips and we just stumble through life, hoping ineffectively for what we could so easily bring into our lives, if we just knew we could.

But don't despair, the magnificent, brave, creative soul you were when you came to earth is still there, and still alive! It's just buried under all that mental junk. It just needs to be found, pulled out and given a little CPR and TLC.

I realize that overturning a lifetime of mental junk food and conditioning is a formidable task. Believe me, I do understand that. I grew up in an extremely rigid fundamentalist religion and when I started to explore the idea that I don't have to live my life on the layaway plan – waiting to die to 'inherit the kingdom of God', I was not only sceptical, I was scared. While now I believe that I chose to become mortal to experience everything life has to offer, that was a huge conceptual leap for me. It was also frightening, after all, 'everything life has to offer' includes joy and sadness, happiness and pain, abundance and loss. But now I understand that life is so much bigger than that.

As humans we have the opportunity to experience life in all its colours and we have the ability to choose our perspective. We can choose to see the world as gray, scary and limited. Or we can view it as though through a kaleidoscope, as an ever-changing rainbow of colors and possibilities. I choose the latter. I choose to adopt a Perspective of Unlimited Possibility. I choose to access my power and become a partner with the Universe in creating the life of my dreams. After all, that's the life I was born to live.

There are two cautions associated with recognizing and using the power that you have as a partner with the Universe. First of all, when you accept this power, you also accept the responsibility. No longer can you let others make your choices or take away your power. When you are the co-creator of your life, you must learn to accept the praise for your greatness as well as the responsibility for your setbacks. But as the co-creator, you always have the choice of how you respond; how you take a situation and turn it into your triumph.

The second caution is that when you have such power you must always be careful to use it only for good. Never use this power to control or meddle in others' lives or to wish harm on another person. Whatever thoughts and energy you send out will come back to you so make sure that you get back only good things by only sending out positive thoughts, words, energy or action.

Your power as a partner with the Universe is an awesome thing—the most exciting challenge that you'll ever accept. Are you up for this challenge? Are you ready to partner with the Universe? Are you ready to access the power of Future Pull?

Connect with the Universe

If you want to find God, hang out in the space between your thoughts
  -Alan Cohen

All religions and all cultures around the world have developed ways to access the power of the Universe. Prayer, meditation, vision quests, chanting, drumming, and sacred dance are just a few of the routes that are commonly taken as people seek to return to their source.

Often the process of connecting with the Universe incorporates some way of helping the individual to enter another level of consciousness. Repetitive prayer, like the rosary, is an example. Repeating a prayer as you finger your rosary or mala beads, allows you to enter a state of 'neutral', to quiet the mind and go deeper inside yourself. Drumming or chanting is another way to move beyond the conscious awareness of your environment.

Vision quests or retreats, where a seeker physically removes him or herself from their usual environment, is a time-honored route to another level of consciousness. Jesus, for example, spent forty days fasting in the wilderness where he not only entered another dimension but had a battle of wills with Satan. I don't believe in Satan but I can certainly believe that even Jesus struggled with his 'inner demons', perhaps doubts and fears and limiting beliefs and thoughts.

Fasting, isolation, drumming, even hallucinogenic drugs have been used to facilitate entry into the spirit world. Or perhaps it would be more accurate to say that these techniques and tools allow a person entry into their true selves.

Rather than thinking of it as leaving your body or visiting some 'other place', think of it as just going deeper into yourself, to the place that is always there, the spirit in you. Doesn't that sound easier? A lot less scary. You don't have to have an out of body experience—you have to have an inner body experience.

Meditation is perhaps the most non-dramatic way to access your greater self. Meditation has no bells and whistles; it can be done anywhere once you learn how, and it's easy to learn. It takes practice but the physical, intellectual, emotional and of course spiritual benefits are well worth a few minutes of sitting still every day.

That's really what meditation is—stillness. It means that you sit (or stand or lie) still, emptying your mind and going deeper into the silence of the spirit deep inside you. Well perhaps it's not quite as easy as that sentence makes it sound. Your mind will immediately start to bounce around, thinking up things to think about and trying to stop you from becoming empty. Your body will start to twitch and itch and cramp.

All of this is normal—in fact there's even a name for the way your mind will try to distract you. It's called 'monkey mind'. If you think of how a monkey bounces around from point to point, swinging from trees, chattering and squealing, you'll certainly understand that label. If you try to wrestle that monkey down and hold it down through sheer willpower, it will fight back and you'll be consumed with trying to maintain control. No, that doesn't work. On the other hand, if you ignore the monkey and turn away, mentally, it will eventually disappear. It will drop in occasionally to see if you want to play but again, ignore it and it will slink away. Then you can go deeper and become still. It is in that stillness that you will find your greater self, the Universe.

Often people say to me, "I can't meditate. I've tried and I just can't do it." After a few more questions, it becomes obvious that what they've done is sit still for a few minutes, tried to empty their mind and then given up in frustration. Meditation is not something that comes easily or naturally. We are too used to the inner dialogue that we have going on all the time. That inner dialogue is what keeps us up at night, stops us from enjoying the 'now', reminds us constantly of all the rules and warnings that we received from our parents and teachers and, most destructively, reinforces any negative message we've ever received.

When I was young, my grandfather would send me comics from England. There was one comic that really caught my imagination and I've often had a little fantasy that my head and body really work in the way that was pictured. There was a large head with a lot of different compartments: the brain compartment, the eyes, the nose, the mouth. Little people lived and worked in these compartments, frantically adjusting and coping as the 'head person' went about his daily life. So the nose people, for example, would test a smell that came in through the nostrils and make a decision as to the source and action required and then send a message, using a series of mouthpieces and chutes to the appropriate department. The eye people would pull levers and chains to make the eyes move in the right direction. The mouth people would work the machinery to make chewing and swallowing happen. And as they all worked, they all carried on conversations and had their own lives. Sometimes when I'm feeling overwhelmed or my inner dialogue is too busy, I think of those little people and how they must be working so hard.

Okay, before you decide that I'm crazy and close this book, I want to assure you that I know that those little people don't really exist. But sometimes, with the amount of inner dialogue that we all have going on, it does feel like it.

In reality, the inner dialogue is more like a tape that has been recorded over the course of our lifetime and that replays conversations or phrases that had a strong impact on us. Sometimes the tape plays so loudly and insistently that all we do is respond. So instead of living a proactive life, we are just reacting to pre-taped messages. Meditation is one way of turning off the tape.

Meditation is a skill and like any skill it has to be learned and practiced. Trying it once and giving up is wimpy! You don't want to be wimpy, do you? Give yourself a month and try it for only a short time perhaps twice a day. Start with a five minute meditation morning and evening and then gradually work up to twenty minutes or half an hour twice a day. I guarantee you that at the end of that month, if you persevere, you will find that meditation becomes an important part of your day.

Create a Compelling Vision

We must be willing to get rid of the life we've planned, so as to have the life that is waiting for us. The old skin has to be shed before the new one can come.
                    -Joseph Campbell

Create a Compelling Vision

Dream lofty dreams, and as you dream, so you shall become. Your vision is the promise of what you shall one day be; your ideal is the prophecy of what you shall at last unveil.
-James Allen

In this section you will create a compelling vision of the life you were meant to live. You'll start by evaluating where you are now and where you want to go. Considering your current circumstances, where you are physically, emotionally, spiritually and intellectually, gives you a starting point–a jumping off point.

You may even find that when you describe your vision of your ideal life—the one that is going to inspire you, fuel your drive, give you energy and pull you effortlessly toward it—and compare it to your current reality, that it's not as far off as you think. You'll be able to appreciate the great and the good in your life right now. Express gratitude for all your blessings and the doors of heaven open up and shower you with more.

In this section, you'll look at your life as you live it now. You'll identify and acknowledge the parts of your life now that you love and want to continue. You'll identify the things that you want to change so that you can clear them, finish them, and get them out of your way. Then you'll visualize the life you want to create, in detail, in all its glory. You'll love that. I guarantee it.

Once you have a vision, you'll create the clear intention statements that will lead you to it and a path to follow as you set out on your journey. You'll create a map that will guide you as you as you step confidently in the direction of your dreams. Not a rigid timed route; you aren't a train and you don't have to be at the station on time. Remember, you're co-creating your life with the Universe and the Universe doesn't use earthly clocks.

This journey is meant to be one of self-discovery, adventure and celebration. It's a bit like a puzzle; sometimes you have to figure out the clues, watch for signposts and be ready to choose between forks in the road. When you have a clear vision that fills you with excitement and joy, it will seem as though you can suddenly see signs that you wouldn't have noticed before. You'll find it easy to make unerring decisions about the right way to go.

So take the time to create a vision that lifts you up, fills you with excitement and passion and keeps you going even when you encounter the odd storm, the rocky road, the steep climb, or the just plain boring bit of hard slogging work. Then, whenever you need to, you can come back here and refresh yourself with the vision of the life of your dreams.

And remember....be brave! Look up and set your sights high! Dream big!

Start From Where You Are

The past is behind, learn from it.
The future is ahead, prepare for it.
The present is here, live it.
    -Thomas S. Monson

No matter where you're heading, you have to start from where you are. In fact, right now, the present moment, is all you have.

Close your eyes for a moment and breathe in. Now hold that breath for a moment before you let it out slowly. One of the lessons inherent in living mindfully is that each breath is, potentially, your last. Paying attention to the here and now recognizes the immense importance of the present moment.

While it's tempting to spend your time daydreaming of your future and working towards your goals, it's really a terrible waste of a life. Your life is made up of the 'now moments'. If you walk through life looking only up ahead at tomorrow, next week, next year, you lose sight of the gift that your life is right here and now.

Some people spend a great deal of time dwelling on the past; chewing on what happened like a cow chews its cud and wishing for what might have been. In reality, your past is what created the magnificent creature that you are right now. Your wisdom is the result of your experience and whether you look back on your past with pleasure or regret, it has led you to the point where you are right now.

I once received an email just at the right moment to help me make a major life decision and move on from a bad situation. It asked me to imagine my life as a book. All of the pages up to right now are written in, filled with the story of my life until now. It contains all the joy, all the pain, all the mistakes, all the triumphs. Then I was asked to imagine turning the page to today and looking down on a beautiful, spotless white page, completely empty. It asked me to consider, did I want to cut and paste from the previous pages? Or did I want to fill the empty pages with a new story? It was a transformative moment. I realized I was in that difficult situation because I kept repeating the same behaviours over and over again. It was such a compelling thought that I immediately got up and made the call I needed to make to end the uncomfortable situation and stop the cycle. Right now, you have that choice. Are you going to cut and paste and repeat your past? Or are you going to write a new story.

That new story starts right now. You can't skip a few pages and start in the future. You start right now to live the life you want to live, to create the life that you were meant to live.

Of course sometimes you have messes that have to be cleaned up to allow the space for your new life. You have to clean out the old to make way for the new. I know someone who has, several times, walked away from his life, leaving it all, everything. Every time he walks away, he leaves everything behind. Last time he left all his family photos, his papers, his clothes, even a jar full of coins that he had saved. He left it all, put a small case with some grooming items, one change of clothing, and a computer in his car and drove away. He cut off all contact with friends and family. He walked away, became a new person and started a new life. That's an extreme case and it certainly can't be easy to start over with absolutely nothing. But even he had some baggage that he couldn't drop. He still had his memories, habits, expectations and regrets. Walking away is not a resolution, coming to peace with your past is.

I'm not suggesting that you spend years in therapy rehashing your childhood, or trying to figure out why you act the way you do. Therapy has it's place and if you have serious issues that need professional intervention, then absolutely seek out that level of help. We have already seen that what we focus on we attract into our lives. Recognize your past, acknowledge its influence and impact on your present, and then refocus on the here and now so that you can move on to a grand new future. Dwelling on what went wrong in the past will only attract more of the same into your life.

Abraham, when speaking through Esther Hicks, has a very neutral way of referring to all the bad 'stuff' in life. He calls it 'contrast'. When we are born into or live in a situation with a lot of 'contrast', like a dysfunctional family, abuse, or poverty, it helps us to identify what we don't want and so move forward to what we do want.

I attended one of the Abraham-Hicks workshops in Toronto and I was impressed by the pace and the sheer quantity of information about the Law of Attraction. Esther invites questions from the audience and then speaks rapidly and very animatedly, responding off the cuff to any and all questions. Often people ask questions about why we have negative things like crime, illness, violence. Abraham always reminds us that we are born into a place of contrast so that we can make a choice about what we want to attract into our life. Less contrast, Abraham says, leads to less change. Great contrast, or more pain, leads to greater change for the better. So rather than regret the amount of 'contrast' in your life, value it, because it acts as a catalyst to propel you into a future of even more positive growth.

There's another reason for starting with the present. This is where you are right now and I'd be willing to bet that it's not all bad. I bet you have some things, people, behaviours, experience, and ideas that you value and you would miss if you left them behind. You may be far closer to living your ideal life than you recognize. Probably the most important part of living a life of joy and happiness is being grateful. In fact, I will continue to bring it up over and over throughout this process. Gratitude should be a daily practice and right here, right now, in the present, you have much to be grateful for.

Take the time to figure out where you are right now so that you can decide where you want to go in the future.

Make Room for Your Future

When one door closes, another door opens, but we so often look so long and so regretfully upon the closed door that we do not see the doors that open for us.
                              -Alexander Graham Bell

Have you ever parked on a steep hill and put on the emergency brake and then later driven away forgetting to take off the brake? I once drove for two days like that, wondering what was wrong with my car, why I had no pick up and go. If you sometimes feel like that, lacking in energy and motivation, it might be because you have your brakes on. Time to take the brakes off.

What is holding you back? It could be many things. Do any of these ring a bell for you–clutter, old unresolved disagreements and hurts, regrets, uncompleted projects, unfulfilled dreams and wishes that you just can't let go of, resentments, bad habits, promises you made and never kept, promises made to you that weren't kept, or old worn out self perceptions and labels.

Your energy and focus are the most important resources you have. Remember, I'll say it again and again, what you focus on is what you are attracting into your life. If you are distracted by 'stuff', physical, mental or emotional, you are looking backward and that's where you'll stay–in the past.

Clutter is a common source of fatigue. When you are surrounded by junk, it's like it drags you down–literally. If all your surfaces are covered with 'stuff' your attention is pulled down when you need to be looking up and forward. I know because clutter is something that I've struggled with and continue to deal with to some extent. I'm a creative person and like many creatives I tend to be easily distracted and take on too many projects. All those projects, aside from the distraction caused by the fact that they are incomplete, create mess. I have boxes of paints and canvasses and a great big easel. I have paper and many many books. I have fabric and beads and 'findings'. I have exercise equipment. And I have a very small house. Bad combination.

I know how challenging it is to clear clutter. I know how it feels to start purging and then reach a point where anxiety starts to set in and you start feeling like you can't throw anything else out. You start to make bad choices about whether you need an item or not because you seem to have reached your limit on purging. It's not all about just finding better ways to organize your stuff; it's really about getting rid of what you don't need any more.

Imagine that every single thing you own is attached to you by a string. Energy flows through that string. If the item is something you love, or need, or is of value to you in some way, the energy flows to you. If it is clutter, the item drains the energy from you. The key is to get rid of the stuff that drains your energy and only keep the things that feed your energy. As you declutter your space, imagine that you are cutting the string from your body and stopping it from draining your energy. As you move through your home or office, cutting off strings attached to clutter, imagine yourself becoming lighter and more energetic. The only things you should keep are those that feed you and increase your energy. Try it.

How about incomplete projects and unfinished business? Do you have half finished sewing projects, half read books, pictures you never hung, boxes of photos to sort and file? Do you have burned out light bulbs? Do you have half finished renovations projects? Do you have unpaid bills collecting late fees every month? Is one of your stove burners not working? One of your doors not quite closing properly? An annoying noise in your car engine that you need to get checked out?

You're busy and I certainly understand that. It can be challenging sometimes to find the time to take care of so many little things. Today we tend to have larger houses, more complex cars, more stuff, and it all has to be cared for. And in spite of the promise that computers would lead to four day work weeks and make life so much easier, in reality we work much longer than we did just a decade ago. In fact, it appears that as we accept the 24/7 connectivity and ability to work from anywhere at any time that is now possible, we will have a blurring of the boundary between work and personal life.

Time becomes 'squishy' and things get left behind or left undone. What we leave behind become our incompletions. They drain our energy and keep us from putting our focus where it will better serve us.

Take the time to go through your house and office, listing all your incompletions and then set aside a short time every day to start getting them done. It won't take long to change that light bulb, but when you do, it's one less drain on your energy.

The emotional incompletions are more challenging. You may be able to take action—make a call, send a card, write a letter—that eliminates some of them. But some may be situations that make you feel sad or regretful and have no easy resolution. For example, you might regret that you never had the chance to say 'I love you' to a person before they passed on. You may have had a disagreement with someone and now have no contact with them and can't resolve it. You may still feel the pain of a lost love and still hold the hope that it can be revived. If you can take some action to resolve the issue, do it now. But do it with the intention of ending the emotional energy drain, not to resuscitate it so that it can continue to consume you.

Some situations just need to be declared dead so that you can bury them and move on. Sometimes we just want to have the last word, ask why something happened, find some reason so that we can understand. Some situations don't have such a clean ending and we have to choose between holding on to it and brooding or freeing ourselves from bondage to it. You may have heard the analogy that holding resentment is like letting someone live in your head rent-free. Time to evict those bad tenants.

I find that a ritual can be helpful in purging those emotional and mental demons. My favourite is to write out a list of the thoughts, regrets, resentments, and outdated self-perceptions that are holding you back and then burn it. As you burn it, say a little prayer of gratitude for all the lessons that the experience brought you and then let go. It may not be instantaneous, but you've set the emotional incompletions free and you can allow them to move out of your life.

Occasionally you may find a lesson in the process. Once I was leading one of my New Years workshops and as part of the clearing process, we wrote out all the things that were holding us back and went outside to burn them. That year I had developed a lingering sore throat and cold in the summer and it had lasted for half a year. By winter I was really feeling wimpy and sickly. I was starting to think of myself as one of those Victorian ladies who are lifetime invalids. So one of the things on my list was my self-perception as a 'sick person'.

It was a bitter cold day and, because we were just outside an office building, the best we could do was to use a small coffee can and burn the papers in the can. Usually I like to have a roaring bonfire and take our time, enjoying the process, but in this case, we didn't have that option. So we had to go one at a time, making a statement about releasing it to the universe, and then burning the paper in the can.

When it was my turn, the paper wouldn't burn. No matter how we tried, my paper wouldn't burn. We were all a little freaked out. People were saying, "Jackie, what does that mean? Why isn't it burning?" I didn't know and I was upset by it too. I ended up tearing it into little pieces but I still felt a little doomed. Right after New Years I suddenly got pneumonia and had to go to the doctor and take antibiotics and take some time off. After that I was fine—no more sore throat or lingering cold. No more self-perception of myself as a 'sickly person'. Perhaps I needed to be forced into taking a time out.

If you let it, clearing can become a long term process; an excuse that prevents you from moving on. Don't wait till all your clutter is gone before you move on to the next step. Don't put off visualizing your ideal day until your emotional baggage is all gone. When you do that, you have just allowed clearing to become another one of the things that are holding you back. Clearing will be an ongoing process, start it, keep on top of it but continue moving ahead into your future.

Your Ideal Day

*Dream no small dreams for they have no
power to move the hearts of men.*
-Goethe

It's time to dream! It's time to create your vision of your ideal life so that the path to reach it can unfold effortlessly. It's time to set the power of Future Pull in motion. This will be fun. Are you ready?

I know that this process works. I've seen it work with many people and I've experienced it myself. I've already described my first successes with the Ideal Day process, when I first started using it and created that clear vision of my future home, dog, vehicle and business. But what about all those people who set goals and work so diligently and fail to accomplish what they set out to do? Perhaps you've found that yourself.

Twenty-five years ago when I first started exploring the ideas and concepts I'm presenting here, I taught various techniques for goal-setting, decision-making, stress management and time management. Some worked and some were disappointing failures.

The usual model for setting and achieving life goals back in those days was something called S.M.A.R.T. This was an acronym, still in use today, that meant goals must always be Specific, Measurable, Achievable, Realistic, and Time-defined. I would go through the accepted process of helping people to come up with realistic, achievable and measurable goals and then to set smaller objectives and timelines for achievement. It was often frustrating to me to see people who were really committed and hard-working, with good hearts and good intentions, setting goals that were

S.M.A.R.T. and plowing towards them relentlessly – and failing.

On the other hand, sometimes I would have clients who would refuse to be what I saw as 'realistic' and, instead of setting the S.M.A.R.T. goals, would resolutely, against my advice, set D.U.M.B. goals. Those are Dogged, Unusual, Mindless, but totalled Believed-In goals. And they would achieve them. In fact, sometimes the circumstances would be amazing or even miraculous. Synchronicity and serendipity would occur. Opportunities would fall into place. And those silly clients who were blindly committed to their dream would achieve things that just seemingly were unachievable.

I felt like a failure myself when I was going by the book, guiding clients through the S.M.A.R.T. process and watching them try so hard, work so hard, and fail miserably. I wanted to help. What made it even more difficult for me, and I'm sure for them as well, was that I was one of those people who had seemingly impossible dreams 'just happening'. Yes, I was one of those dreamers who set D.U.M.B. goals and achieved them, while trying to convince others that they needed to be S.M.A.R.T. If I could do it for myself, why couldn't I help others?

I had one friend in particular that I cared about very much and I watched him struggle and strive toward his goals. No one could have worked harder! In spite of physical and emotional stress and challenges he persevered and worked endlessly every single day. It was like he was struggling up an endless mountain with a heavy pack on his back, slipping back every few steps on loose rocks. He never made progress but always kept trying. He was the essence of S.M.A.R.T. and it just didn't work. Why not?

I started to take a good look at those who achieved dreams, even amazing dreams, against all odds and sometimes without a great deal of struggle. I compared them with people who set goals by the book, laid out their objectives, set tasks to accomplish them and did all the things they needed to do when they needed to do it. I discovered the key to achieving your dreams without effort.

Remember, my first Ideal Day and how it all came true? Well it didn't ALL come true. My first Ideal Day had me living on the West coast by the ocean. Since I had family and friends on Vancouver Island who wanted me to move there, that wouldn't even have been an unrealistic goal to aspire to, but I didn't achieve it. So why did I not achieve it? That was the one part of my Ideal Day that didn't come to pass. Looking back, I believe it was because I was conflicted about it. It wasn't really my dream – it was the dream of my friends and family that I had assumed.

I like living by water. In fact, I live right by the largest inland lake in the world. Because my friends and family were on the coast, I was trying to incorporate that into the vision of my future that I was creating. But the problem was, there were some real negatives for me about living out there. I didn't like the idea of living on an island, with ferry line-ups to get to the mainland, too much family (which can definitely be a plus or a minus), and earthquakes! And then the big one – my son would be all the way across the country! When you are conflicted about your dreams, when they are other people's dreams rather than your own, the pull isn't there and you probably won't achieve them.

The other key as to whether your dream is powerful enough to pull you is whether you believe you can have it or believe you deserve it. The belief and intent have to be whole-hearted, not buried in doubt, for it to pull you.

If you set the goal of winning the lottery, and you focus on that and use all of the tools introduced in this guide, you may still have an inkling of doubt about your ability to really win the lottery. After all, you hear the odds all the time. You've bought tickets before and won nothing. I've already mentioned that the odds of winning a lottery of over $15 million are lower than your odds of being struck by lightning. These thoughts are enough of a wet blanket to douse your flame of intent and destroy the power of Future Pull.

If you set a goal for yourself that you don't really believe you deserve or are worthy of, the same thing happens. You may set that goal and try to keep your eye on it but if, in your heart, you believe that you are aspiring too high, you subconsciously lower your sights. You are no longer focused on your dream. You are looking down and have distracted yourself from your real dream. I believe that was the problem for my friend. He didn't really believe he deserved the outcome he was striving for and he let his focus waver.

Your vision has to have several key ingredients for it to become the powerful Future Pull that you want. It has to be yours and yours alone; it has to be something you believe is possible and that you believe you are worthy of, and it has to be unconflicted.

Meet those conditions and you will find that it becomes effortless to move towards your vision. Frank Lloyd Wright said, "The thing always happens that you really believe in and the belief in the thing makes it happen."

Creating your Ideal Day may happen easily or it may take you a period of time. Don't force it. Start by allowing yourself to daydream. Just let your imagination go and visualize what your life would be like if you were living the life you were born to live.

Close your eyes and let yourself see how a typical day would unfold in your future ideal life. Start from when you first open your eyes in the morning. Look around and clearly see the room you are in. What do you hear? Do you hear birds singing in the trees? A nearby creek bubbling over the rocks? Or perhaps a rooster's cry wakes you up. It's your life to create.

What do you do when you first wake up? Are you filled with excitement? Do you jump out of bed and immediately start your day? Or do you stretch and relax for a while before you get up? Do you have a partner lying beside you? Or are you alone? Do children run in and jump on your bed to wake you? It's your life to create.

As your mind's eye moves through your day, pay attention to the details. Where do you live? What do the rooms look like? Where do you work? Who do you work with? How do you spend your work day? How do you feel as you interact with your coworkers and the public? What skills are you using? How does the time flow in your Ideal Day? What about the evening? How do you spend it? Do you have a hobby that allows you to express your creativity? Do you work out or perhaps take a jujitsu or zumba dance class? Do you spend the evening with friends at a restaurant or entertaining them in your own kitchen? It's your life to create.

As you follow your future self moving through your Ideal Day, pay attention to the feelings you experience. If you feel any hesitation or discomfort or doubt it might be an indication that the details are not authentic. Remember, you want this Ideal Day to be yours and yours alone. Not a day that is imposed on you by someone else's expectations. It should fill you with joy and optimism.

When you've clearly seen your Ideal Day in your mind, it's time to record it. There is a very specific way to write it out.

First, write it in the first person. So you would say, "I wake up early to the sound of the ocean waves breaking on the beach outside my home." Or, "I meet friends for lunch at the local bistro and we sit and enjoy our salads and chat for a couple of hours."

Second, write it in the present tense as though it's happening right now. You would write something like, "I am working out intensely while my personal trainer makes sure that I push myself and give it that extra push." Or, "Now that it's eleven o'clock at night and my guests have left, my husband and I clean up the dishes and go hand in hand up to bed."

Third, describe the details. You might write, "My office is large and airy and uncluttered and I have a view of the city from the floor to ceiling windows." Or, "I enjoy driving my Toyota Avalon along the highway, window open and the dog sitting in the back seat enjoying the breeze."

Another option is to write it out as though it's the end of your Ideal Day and you are writing in your journal. Or turn it into a letter that you are writing to a friend telling them how your day went. The important thing is to make it real, make it vivid, and make it as though it is happening or has happened. You are creating your future reality.

One final caution: Don't let 'what's possible' limit your dreams. Let your imagination go free. Mike Dooley, one of the teachers on *The Secret*, and author of *Leveraging the Universe and Engaging the Magic*, refers to the 'cursed hows'. Don't let the 'cursed hows' muddy your waters. Just picture, as clearly as you can, the life you would create if you had no barriers, no limits.

One of the most inspiring people I spoke with about how she made her dreams come true was Zenovia Evans. Zenovia grew up in 'the hood' in New York City. Her mother was a crack addict and abandoned Zenovia when she was just a baby. Her father was a good man but uneducated and lost. He wasn't able to provide Zenovia with much structure or direction as she was growing up so she ran the streets with all the other lost kids. But Zenovia was different—she had dreams and she believed in them. In fact, Zenovia still has the loose-leaf binder that she made when she was young. She would write out exactly how she wanted her life to be when she grew up. She'd make lists of her goals and add to it as new possibilities were revealed to her.

When Zenovia graduated from high school, she left for Atlanta and never looked back. When I spoke to her she was just a week from her twenty-ninth birthday, an attorney in Colorado and the author of the E-book series, *J.D. Lifeline: A Law School Guide for the New Legal Economy.* Zenovia still writes out her Ideal Day and goals. In fact, she writes them out in full every day, in longhand, on a yellow legal pad, adjusting and revising as she fine-tunes her vision.

There's a good reason for writing out your Ideal Day in long-hand. When I talked to Barbara Schiffman, co-author with Camille Leon of *The Exhilaration Effect, Building the Courage to Take Your Leap of Faith*, she told me that the process of hand-writing forges new links in the brain, making whatever you are writing more believable and more achievable. So rather than sitting at the computer typing out your Ideal Day, try writing it out in your journal. Then, every time you have a new idea, or an even more exciting detail that adds to the realism, write it out again.

The visualization process is crucial to the Future Pull process. That is how you create the reality up ahead in the future that pulls you in the right direction. I suggest that you make it part of a daily practice. Each day spend some time—ten or fifteen minutes—clearly visualizing your Ideal Day in all its glorious detail. Use all your senses. Hear the birds, smell the coffee, feel the smooth sheets when you first wake up. Talk to a friend as you take a stroll in the park, smell your partner's cologne or aftershave as you dance, hear the thwack of the golf club hitting the ball, feel the breeze on your skin as you skim the waves in your future sailboat.

Are you ready to day dream? Go for it! Spend some time in the future, fully enjoying the life of your dreams, and then record it on paper. Do one or do several, it's your life to create.

You May Be Closer Than You Think

Nothing happens unless first we dream.
                              -Carl Sandberg

In the last chapter, you described your Ideal Day. If you made a list of the elements of your Ideal Day that are essential, important or just nice to have, how close is your Ideal Day to your current reality? You may find that you are much closer than you expected. Surprisingly, pieces of your dreams and desires may have already found their way into your life.

Comparing the present with your Ideal Day will show you what is right with your life right now and helpnhjn you gain some perspective about how far you have to travel towards the life you want to create in the future. Those things that are right with your life right now will be an important source of energy and satisfaction as you continue to pull your Future towards you. But not if you discount them and take them for granted.

For example, if you find that in your Ideal Day you wake up in a pale blue room that is uncluttered and peaceful, and you actually do wake up every morning in a room just like that, do you appreciate that blessing? Do you recognize that that element of your Ideal Day already exists? Do you show gratitude for it in the here and now?

Perhaps in your Ideal Day you are spending quality time with your children, reading them a story before bed every night and hearing their prayers. Do you do that now? Can you do that now? It would make your Ideal Day that much more of a reality.

One example that hits home for me is related to watching television. In my Ideal Day, I don't even know if I have a television. It certainly isn't part of the environment that I view as I walk through my day and I don't spend any time, no matter how many Ideal Days I do, laying on the couch watching reality television.

In my Ideal Day I spend my time writing, coaching clients, enjoying the company of friends, painting, and sitting in front of the fireplace reading and listening to the radio. I could do all of those things right now! I don't have to wait for the Future to flow into my life bringing my Ideal Day for those aspects of my ideal life to come to a reality. It's just a matter of remembering and taking action, and then appreciating the parts of my life that are exactly right, right now.

Set Clear Intentions

*Every great dream begins with a dreamer.
Always remember, you have within you the
strength, the patience, and the passion to reach
for the stars, to change the world.*
-Harriet Tubman

You've designed your Ideal Day and you've identified what you really really really want, what you want but can live without, and what would just be the icing on the cake. You've also compared your Ideal Day to your real, right now life and you have seen just how close you are. I hope you're expressing daily gratitude for all the blessings you have right now, and I hope you're making the most of them, no longer taking them for granted while pining for what you don't yet have.

But what about the gaps? What about the elements of your Ideal Day that are missing? Now is the time to identify them and turn them into a list so that you can start attracting them into your life. Now is the time to create your bucket list – the list of what you want to do, what you want to have, where you want to go, and what you want to learn before you kick the bucket.

In the 2007 movie, *Bucket List*, Jack Nicholson and Morgan Freeman played two terminally ill men who decide to attack their bucket lists and check off everything they have on the lists. They climb mountains; they jump out of airplanes; they stay in expensive penthouse suites. You may have a whole list of adventures you want to try. You may have places to see, things to do, stuff to get, people to meet. It's your list to create.

My bucket list includes seeing New Orleans and visiting the butterfly farm in Florida. I'd also like to kayak near an iceberg, write a book, and meet Richard

Branson. My list also includes some goals that I've already accomplished like flying a plane, kayaking with Orcas, and getting a big flat screen tv. Those things make reading my list even more enjoyable. They are evidence that I've accomplished some of my goals and that I can achieve even more. My bucket list is organic, ever changing. I read it regularly and sometimes I've changed my mind about something and I take it off the list. Sometimes I add new things or revise the items I have to make them more specific.

It's important to be specific. In fact, it sometimes seems to me that it's only when you do get specific that the Universe says, "Okay I get it now. You want that! Okay, here it is."

In February 1997, after watching a documentary about retirement savings and pensions, my friend and I were discussing the financial needs we would have before we could retire. Having been mostly self-employed and occasionally rather lax in my retirement investments, I commented that in order to retire I would have to either win the lottery or grow my business to a million dollars in value and then sell it. I said that I'd probably have a better chance with growing and selling my business and that, yes, that would be my plan. I declared that I would grow it to $500,000 by the end of that year.

Now at that time, I had a full-time job and was operating my business on a part-time, home-based basis. My friend laughed and suggested I lower my sights a bit for that year.

I replied, "Okay then if you insist, $100,000 by the end of this year. $500,000 by the end of next year." We both laughed.

However, so much can change in just a few short months. I was laid off from my job at the end of March and by the end of December, my business had $100,000 in federal contracts. By the end of January 1998, just a year after our conversation, I had exactly $475,000 in contracts and I had jumped from a sole owner, home based business to a small company with twelve employees. Never underestimate the power of a clear intention.

Intention is a powerful thing. Combined with passion it is virtually unstoppable. Intention is more than just wishing; it's more than wanting; it's more than affirmation. It leaves no other option than to attain what you focus your attention on. Intention leaves no doubt. Intention is not wishy-washy.

Intention has power. When you intend to do something, you let the world know, "Get out of my way. I'm coming through and what I want to happen is going to happen."

In the workshop he did with Dr. Deepak Chopra, *How to Get What You Really, Really, Really, Really Want*, Dr. Wayne Dyer lists four stages or levels that lead to manifesting your desires. Level one is wishing. Wishing is when you start to daydream about an idea or a goal. You wish for more prosperity or for love or for a new car. Wishing is a wisp of a thought. It's a first step.

Level two is wanting. Wanting is when you desire something enough to ask for it. Just asking out loud, clearly and without equivocation can be enough to bring something into reality.

In every one of the Gospels, it tells us that Jesus said that if you ask, you will receive.[1] Prayer is about asking (but don't forget it's also about thanking). Prayer is at level two and prayer alone is a powerful thing. Prayer has been the subject of medical research and some studies have shown that even long distance prayer by strangers can affect the healing process positively. In fact, and I've now mentioned this several times, asking is so powerful that you should always be careful what you ask for because, without a doubt, you will get it.

An intention is at level three. An intention moves beyond 'I wish' or 'I want' or 'Will you help me'. An intention is energy and when you intend you send that energy out into the Universe to make something happen. As one of the participants in one of my workshops said, "It's as if once you have a vision and the

---

[1] Matthew 21:22; Mark 11:24; Luke 11:9; John 15:7. These are just a few. There are actually numerous scriptures that say the same thing; an indication to me that this is one of the statements that Jesus probably did actually make.

intention to achieve it, all the energies of the Universe conspire to make it happen."

Isn't that a powerful thought? The idea that once you have a vision and the intention to achieve it, all of the energies of the Universe conspire to make it happen means that you have truly started to work in concert with the Universe. You really have begun to co-create the life of your dreams.

Level four is when you add passion to your intention. Dr. Wayne Dyer calls it 'hardening of the will'. Passion is when you are single-minded and cannot be deterred from achieving what you want.

I use intention on a continual basis, setting intentions for my days as well as the bigger view of my future. Sometimes, when I set an intention for the way I want my day to unfold, it plays out so accurately that I can't help but be surprised, even though I know that intention works. For example, a few weeks ago I was in Toronto and I had to travel from my hotel to a building in a complex that I wasn't familiar with. Before I started my day, I wrote the following in my blog:

I have to go out now and navigate the transit system. I can't tell you how easily I get lost. I choose to believe that it's because I'm left-handed. My son thinks it's because I'm missing a part of my brain—I don't know how it was supposed to have gone missing. I have to take the subway, then a bus and then walk (WALK!) to some big complex where I have to find a building A and then wait to be escorted in. And I have to be there by a deadline. That deadline is 45 minutes from now so I better get going.

I am setting an intention—two intentions—for my day and I expect that it will all work out perfectly:

1. I am going to get 10 more Twitter followers to keep me on my goals to reach 150 by April 1.

2. I am going to have a smooth enjoyable journey to my destination. The subway will be

on time and not crowded. I will get to sit down. The bus will arrive as soon as I get to the stop—but no sooner so I don't have to run. I will know when to get off, either because I will ask the driver to tell me or I will have a miraculous revelation probably triggered by the bell-toned woman who announces each stop. I will get off the bus and—lo! there will be my colleagues right there heading to the same building so that I can just follow them.

Okay a third intention:

3. I will be smart and wide-awake all day and will learn a lot. And then I'll go and buy that Fossil purse I saw.

It's going to be a great day.

Obviously I believe that an intention has to be very specific, especially when related to getting somewhere that I'm not familiar with. My day did turn out to be great. Later that night, I wrote:

Update: Well did my intentions work? They worked to a miraculous degree—well, one is still playing out.
1. I have 7 new twitter followers so far today. The day is not over and I only need three more! (I ended up with 11 by the end of the day)
2. The subway was fine and I had a seat within two stops. Oh yeah, and the subway was there just as I reached the platform and I didn't have to run. Then the bus arrived at the station just after I arrived so I didn't have to run. Both of them did. First I went to the bus going eastbound and the driver directed me to the right bus. That one also arrived right after I got there and when I got on there was Bharthi, my colleague, who signalled me over and gave me a seat. That was very kind of her and because my knees are so sore from so much walking, I accepted. So she knew exactly where we were going and all was

well. Then on the way back, all of us took the same bus and it was easy and fun to travel together.

3. I was wide awake and bright all day. I learned a lot and quite enjoyed it. On the way home I decided to go straight to the mall to get the purse. I had started thinking I would see if it came in different colors instead of getting the yellow one and I found one in a nice brown but it had goop on it. But it was just gum and I could easily get that off so I asked if I could get a price cut - $25 off the $115 Fossil purse.

So all in all, it was a great day....as intended.

Last week I was in Ottawa for the entire week, travelling by transit to and from a training program. Every day I intended that I would have a seat on the bus no matter how crowded it was, and every day I had a seat.

So what makes the difference between a wish and an intention? An intention is clear and focused and it has energy. When you state an intention you must state it as though there is absolutely no doubt that it will come through. Imagine if you went into a restaurant for dinner and when you placed your order you said, "Oh, I wish I could have the poached salmon on rice." The server would probably be confused as to whether it was what you were really wanting or whether you were just fanaticizing about something that you, for some reason, couldn't order. No, you would say, in a clear voice so there'd be no doubt or confusion, "I'd like the poached salmon on rice, thank you."

You can add power to your intention by using visualization. Clearly state what you wish to happen and then see it unfolding in your mind's eye. For example, imagine that you are going to present an idea at a team meeting. You've done your work and you're ready to present. State the intention that you wish to happen, perhaps something like, "I am going to present my idea in a clear, compelling and confident way and have great answers to any questions that come up. The team will really like it and approve it. I'm so excited to have this opportunity." Then close your eyes for just a few seconds and see yourself standing confidently, smiling around at the team, speaking firmly and enthusiastically. See everyone nodding and smiling as they give you the go ahead.

Start with small every day intentions and as you feel the power of your will, you'll become more confident and even more effective in setting intentions. Don't forget to express gratitude as you receive all the blessings you intend.

A Visual Prayer

Knowledge is limited. Imagination encircles the world
                                              -Albert Einstein

One of the biggest 'Wow!' moments in the movie, *The Secret*, was when John Assaraf described his experience with attracting his dream home with a vision board. He had just moved into a home he had been renovating for a year and his son found his vision boards and asked him what they were. As he showed his son the boards, he realized that he had actually unknowingly bought the very house that he had put on his vision board five years before.

A vision board is a pictoral representation of your Ideal Day. Sometimes they are called treasure maps. I like to think of vision boards as visual prayers. By going through the process of looking for, sorting and arranging images of exactly what you want to attract into your life, you send a request out to the Universe. Along with our words, our thoughts and our feelings, it's another way to create that compelling vision up there in the future.

Over the years, leading workshops to help people clarify and attract their ideal life, I have seen many examples of vision boards working in stunning ways. In 2001, I went to Indiana to take a feng shui practitioners course. I travelled back through Minneapolis and, because I had a layover, I went to dinner at the home of Susan, a new friend I had met at the training. Susan showed me her 'treasure map' and told me the story of how it had come true.

After a major life change, Susan had moved to Minneapolis and was looking for a new home. She had her heart set on a particular condo but there were no units available and, in fact, they were too expensive for her budget anyway. But she took a photo of herself standing in front of the building and added it to her treasure map. She continued to look for a place and checked in regularly to see if any units had come available in her preferred condo building.

As it turned out, the condo board began to have issues and people started moving out. The price of units in the building dropped sharply and she was able to pick up one at a very reasonable price.

Immediately after she bought it, the issues were resolved and the prices returned to their previous level. But the most surprising part of the story is that after she moved in and as she was hanging her treasure map, she realized she had ended up with the exact condo unit that was behind her in the photo she had taken.

I've heard many examples just like this that have convinced me that visual prayers are powerful tools that can help you attract exactly what you desire into your life.

Creating a visual prayer is easy and fun. Just go through magazines and cut out pictures, words, and images that depict the future you'd like to attract into your life. Again, be careful what you wish for. I've seen people put pictures of messy rooms up on their vision board to remind them to declutter. The Universe doesn't work that way. If you put a picture of clutter on your vision board, you can be sure that your clutter will be there to stay. Instead, choose a picture of a serene, clear, uncluttered room and attract that into your life.

You can also put words, quotes and poems on your vision board. Back in 2004, when I first heard the term 'Future Pull', I tried to buy the domain name, futurepull.com, but it was not available. I printed it out on the computer in a large font and put it on my vision board. In about 2007 I had the urge to check it out again and sure enough it was available. I am now the owner of the futurepull.com domain name.

However, one year I cut out a short verse topped by a picture of a ship in a storm. The verse said something like, 'I am not afraid of stormy weather because

I've learned to steer my own ship'. Well, that year was one of great upheaval in my life and I certainly had the opportunity to test my ability to stay afloat. Now I am much more careful about the images and words that I choose to add to my visual prayer.

You can mount your pictures on a foam board, poster board, bulletin board, or even stretched canvas so that you can hang it easily. I have a vision board on stretched canvas that I hang near my front door so that I see it when I leave the house in the morning. I also have a vision book, a large photo album with clear plastic pages that I slip pictures into. I keep that by my bed so that I can look through it before I go to sleep.

Previously, I introduced you to Alex Summer, a young British man I spoke to about his manifestation experiences. Alex has a unique approach to vision boarding. He calls it cosmic ordering and he puts a great deal of thought and planning into it. Alex creates a vision calendar using a desktop publishing program.

Alex says he likes to make it easy for the Universe so he starts by making up lists of what he wants to manfest in his life in the next year and then puts them in the most logical or natural order for achievement. For example, he thought it might be better to have his job become permanent before he tried to get a new apartment so he put them in that order on his vision calendar. Then he asked himself, "When would be the best time to begin a new relationship?" The obvious answer was Valentine's Day so a new girlfriend became part of his February vision. He met his girlfriend on February 10th at a party that he normally would not have attended.

Alex believes that one of the reasons why sometimes people don't succeed at attaining their dreams is because they go outside the 'sphere of availability'. If what they want is too far from their reality, they cannot believe in it as completely as they could if was more attainable. Alex believes that the key is to gradually expand your sphere of availability as you continually set and achieve your dreams.

I think that visual prayers work in several ways. First of all, the process of creating one helps you to be clear about what you want to attract into your life. It's also a personal reminder that acts like a guide so that when you are making any decisions that affect your life, you are unconsciously guided by the memory of your vision board. It can be as minor as choosing a piece of furniture or a piece of jewellery. If you have a picture of the home you want to live in or the way you want to dress on your vision board, you will choose items that are in line with the life you've depicted on your vision board. Of course, it's also a way of letting the Universe know, clearly, what you want to bring into your life. The Universe responds by making it available to you, sometimes in unexpected ways.

After interviewing successful manifesters, I am inclined to believe that having it on display and looking at it every day is not necessarily the source of the vision board power. Just creating it can be action enough.

In one of my New Years workshops, where we visualized our Ideal Day and created a vision board, one of the participants left her vision board in the workshop area. I put it aside to give to her next time I saw her but forgot and there it stayed for the rest of the year.

Karen, unlike most people, didn't fill her vision board with pictures. She preferred to keep it very sparse but put a great deal of effort into choosing just the right images. That year she had a large picture in the middle of a man and woman dancing. In one corner of the poster there were two people playing golf; in another there was a sailboat in front of a large setting sun; in another corner there was a log cabin and in the last corner was a red car under a label saying 'gift'.

At that time the group would get together in July to just touch base and compare notes on how our year was going. That year, Karen told us she was going to move away. She really wanted to manifest a loving relationship with a man and she was ready to look for better hunting grounds. However, at our usual New Years workshop, she was still in town.

We always started off by reviewing our previous year's vision board and relating how the year rolled out. I had forgotten till that point that I still had Karen's board and as she started to tell us her exciting news, I was stunned.

I went and got her board and we all looked at it in amazement. It made the hair on our arms stand up. There was her life – right there on the vision board. She had met a wonderful man at a charity golf tournament. Before the round was over he had asked her to leave early and go for a sunset cruise on his sailboat. He had a beautiful home with white broadloom and a spiral staircase that went up to a loft that overlooked the lake. He also had a log cabin in a nearby quaint village on Lake Superior. At that point, the only thing missing was the red car, but that showed up a few years later when a relative left it to her.

Not surprisingly, I'm a firm believer in the value and magic of vision boards. You will be too when you experience it for yourself.

Choose Your Touchstone

Dreams are the touchstones of our character.
                                  -Henry David Thoreau

The word touchstone has several meanings. In times past, a touchstone was a dark stone, such as basalt or jasper that was used to test the quality of gold or silver. From that came the more common meaning, that of a reference point from which to evaluate the quality or excellence of something.

A touchstone can be a personal symbol or emblem that represents your dream and that helps you to stay on track and stay true to your vision. Throughout the centuries, indigenous people on every continent have used 'medicine bags' in a similar way.

In 1991, hikers found the body of Otzi the Iceman, a man who had frozen to death high in the Italian Alps over 5,000 years ago. He was almost perfectly preserved and, based on his tattoos, clothing and medicine bag, one of the theories is that he was a shaman who had been on a vision quest or carrying out some mystical or ceremonial ritual when he was overtaken by bad weather. His medicine bag carried objects very similar to those that would be carried by a modern day Native American.

The term 'medicine' in this context refers to anything related to the spirit world, Medicine bags provide guidance, healing and protection for their owners. The bags or pouches can be leather, are often decorated with beads, and contain items such as quartz crystals, feathers, plants, or shells. The items in a medicine bag represent the wearer and are often gathered as part of a vision quest.

Your own touchstone or 'medicine' should be something meaningful to you, something that has special significance or resonates with you. I'm sure you've had the experience of finding a small item, perhaps a rock, leaf, flower or shell that seemed to be just waiting for you to pick it up and carry it home. Then when you get it there you have no idea what to do with it. Such a finding might become your touchstone.

Oak leaves have always had special significance for me. The feng shui practitioners program I took was held in the middle of a beautiful oak forest in Indiana. It was fall of 2001 and as I strolled through the woods in the early morning or evening, oak leaves would be gently falling all around me. During one session on nature spirits we were sent out to 'talk to the nature sprites'.

That was while I was still a part of a very strict fundamentalist religion and I was very uncomfortable with the possibility of connecting with demons. Not only that, I just felt plain stupid, talking to sprites – really! But I went out to look for a sprite anyway, even though I had no idea how to recognize one. Were they like leprechauns? Not seeing any little people, I strolled up to a majestic oak tree and tried to start a conversation.

I said, "So, ummmm, hi. I'd like a really nice leaf if you'd send me one down. Thanks."

The tree sent a leaf fluttering down on me. I picked it up, looked at it and let it drop. Ungratefully, I said, 'That one has a hole in it. Could I get another one?"

Now I am shamed by that cavalier attitude, but at the time I really wasn't taking it seriously. In fact, if truth be told, I was making fun of the whole woodland sprites thing. I noticed a nice clump of leaves hanging on the other side of the tree and I headed over only to get attacked by a thorn bush and quite tangled up. When I wrestled myself free, already thinking, "Oh oh, I'm being punished", I gave up and headed down to the pond to lie on the hammock.

When we were called back to the group to discuss our experiences communicating with the sprites, I told my story and everyone went, "Oooooh. That's not good." Which is just about the way I was feeling by then. I just kept thinking about that commercial and the catch phrase, 'It's not nice to fool Mother Nature.'

A week later, as the program came to an end, we all said goodbye and gave each other final messages and hugs. One person gave me a beautiful oak leaf which I wrapped carefully in my luggage and still keep today hanging from a ribbon.

I live in an area where we don't have a lot of oak trees but later that winter, when I was going through a time of decision, I was walking to my car and suddenly, sitting on top of the snow, perfectly clean and unbroken was a small oak leaf. I looked around but I couldn't see an oak or any tree at all, anywhere around. I picked it up and remembered the message I received with the oak leaf I was given, "People throw away what they could have had by insisting on perfection, which they cannot have, and looking for it where they cannot find it."

An oak leaf has become one of my touchstones, reminding me to be grateful for what I have and not to disregard the beauty in every day life while I wait for my future to show up.

When choosing your own touchstone make it meaningful to you. Select something that will inspire you and reorient you to your dream every time you touch it or see it.

It could relate to one of the goals you've already achieved, a reminder of what you have already accomplished and that you have the strength and the commitment to reach your goals. For example, years ago, I used to ask people in workshops to describe what success meant to them. The example I gave was that always having fresh flowers in my house would be my sign of success. Fresh flowers could become my touchstone. I could buy flowers every week, and then as I arrange them and place them just so on my coffee table, I would be reminded that I'm already a success. I would be encouraged to stay on track and achieve even more.

Your touchstone might be a picture or a drawing that you create just for this purpose. I have such a drawing. It's like my own personal logo. It's a line drawing that looks vaguely like a person reaching up toward the sky with one hand, and down toward the ground with the other. I pulled it from the Major Arcana tarot card, The Magician, and it represents pulling down the power of the Universe and turning it into reality here on earth. If it was my touchstone I could draw it and put it on books, my journal, on my monitor, or even on my door so that I would be constantly reminded to stay true to my dream.

Your touchstone might be small object. In the movie, *The Secret*, there was a story about someone who used a small rock as a touchstone.   As a kayaker, I used to love to walk along isolated beaches, picking up beautiful rocks. Actually, a love of rocks must be very common because all of us in the group would have kayaks much lower in the water on the return trip due to all the rocks in the bottom. For years I had those rocks in a bowl in my house. Now I have them all around the fireplace in my backyard including a large one engraved with the word 'Friends'.

If you are a religious person, you may have a medal or sacramental object that would act as a touchstone for you. A particular word might be particularly meaningful for you. If so, you could use that word as a touchstone, writing it in your calendar or journal, using it as a screensaver, or using it as a mantra to help you meditate.

You can use your touchstone as a reminder as you try to control your thinking or change behaviour. For example, let's say you are trying to eliminate negative thinking, perhaps by trying the Seven Day Mental Diet that was developed back in the 30s by Emmet Fox. Wear a stretchy or easily removable bracelet and every time you have a negative thought, change it over to your other wrist. It's a way of becoming aware of your thoughts and taking action to get back on track.

Your touchstone is uniquely yours to choose. Use it to as a way of keeping your vision front and centre as you move steadily towards your future.

Your Daily Practice

Practice means to perform, over and over again in the face of all obstacles, some act of vision, of faith, of desire. Practice is a means of inviting the perfection desired.
-Martha Graham

When I interviewed people all over the world about their experiences with the Law of Attraction, I began to see a common thread. Many of them had a daily practice that helped them to keep their vision clear and bright in front of them.

These daily practices were as varied as the individuals who created them. Some were morning rituals that started the day off with resetting the intention. Some were end of day practices like writing a gratitude list. One thing that was common to all of them was the importance that the practitioners placed on their daily practice.

Michelle Tucker is one person I spoke to who has a morning ritual. She starts with meditation and then voices an open prayer, expressing trust that whatever she is waiting for is on its way to her, saying thank you and instilling a 'knowing' in her heart that her vision is fully formed and waiting for her.

Michelle uses a magnetic photo album for her visual prayer. She is constantly surprised when not only do the images in her vision book show up in her life, they are always right on the money. For example, long before she met her husband, she had a picture of the engagement ring she wanted. When her future husband asked her to marry him and presented her with a ring, it was almost identical to the one in her vision book.

Edie Weinstein, a freelance writer, starts her day by setting an intention before she even gets out of bed. Her intention is very simple—it's to connect with amazing people and have extraordinary experiences. In the realm of amazing people, the Dalai Lama is right up there and Edie was able to manifest a meeting with the Dalai Lama himself.

Although, as religious editor with the Philadelphia Enquirer, she had interviewed famous spiritual and thought leaders, including Jack Canfield and Michael Beckwith, the Dalai Lama seemed to be out of her reach. She admits that even after working behind the scenes for ten years to make her dream come true, when it finally happened, she was overcome with doubt and suffered from the 'Imposter Syndrome'. She had asked and been turned down for an interview several times but never gave up or let go of her dream. So when she found out that the Dalai Lama was coming to Philadelphia, she asked yet again, only to again be told there was no chance.

Only two weeks before the event, she received a call. She was told she could set aside the time during his visit and perhaps she'd be able to talk to him. In the end, she was one of only two people permitted an interview. Edie always says, "Delays are not denials. You must always be prepared to step up to the plate when the Universe presents the opportunity."

Mary Pitman not only has an evening ritual, she turned it into a product that is available on her My Spiritual Affirmations website. Mary was stuck, procrastinating and mired in doubt. Mary had invented a new type of window blind that would keep out the heat and keep the warmth in. She knew what she had to do to take it to market, she was being presented with help, people and opportunities, but she just wasn't taking action. So she came up with affirmations and, with the help of a musician friend, set them to music and turned them into cd's to be listened to before bed or in the morning. Listening to her affirmations as part of a daily practice helped her to overcome her hesitation and get moving on her dream.

To create your own daily practice, choose a time that works for you and make it a sacred part of your day. It might be as simple as sitting quietly with a cup of tea when you first wake, looking through your vision book and setting an intention for the day. Or perhaps evening works better for you. Then you may want to turn the lights down, light a candle, review your day and recognize and give thanks for all the blessings you received.

You can even set aside a special place for your daily practice, creating an altar where you keep reminders of your dream. That might be a touchstone, your vision board, a photograph, your Ideal Day writing, or a journal. It could be in your house or even outside in a sheltered spot. Perhaps your ideal sacred place is a quiet spot under a tree where you can see the sun rise.

I have a chair halfway down my garden right beside the lilac bush, where I have a tall chair and a small table with a candle in a glass container. My chair faces the rising sun and sitting there creating a vision of how I want my day to unfold is a perfect way to start my morning. Unfortunately, because I live in an area where the temperature on a winter morning can drop to minus 30 degrees, it's strictly a summer place for me. Sitting in front of my fireplace in the evening, with quiet music in the background, and writing in my gratitude journal is my favourite winter ritual.

What would be the ideal setting for your daily practice? What rituals will you create to help you stay focused on your dream? It is up to you because it's your personal daily practice. Take the time to make it perfect for you and then do it, and keep on doing it.

Take Inspired Action

*I have learned, that if one advances
confidently in the direction of his dreams,
and endeavours to live the life he has
imagined, he will meet with a success
unexpected in common hours*
-Henry David Thoreau

Take Inspired Action

*Twenty years from now you will be more
disappointed by the things that you didn't do
than by the ones you did do. So throw off the
bowlines. Sail away from the safe harbour.
Catch the trade winds in your sails.
Explore. Dream. Discover*
　　　　　　　　　　　　-Harriet Tubman

Congratulations! You have created a compelling vision of your ideal life that is waiting for you just up ahead. Now Future Pull can be engaged and you will be pulled effortlessly towards the life you were meant to live. Now you can just relax, sit back and wait for UPS, the Universal Postal Service, to drop off all the goodies you've asked for. Right?

Wrong! If you've created a vision of your ideal life that is in line with your authentic self and the life you were meant to live, if you believe in your dream with your whole heart, recognize your power to attract it into your life, and stay focused, the miracle of Future Pull will be engaged. But remember, it's all about working in concert with the Universe.

You are a partner with the Universe and you have to do your share. Engaging the power of the Universe and Future Pull to roll out the path to the future you have created makes it easier. You will be pulled in the right direction. You will have guidance. But you still have to get up and walk the path to your dream.

One of the criticisms of the movie, *The Secret*, was that it implied that all you had to do was ask and you would receive. They used the example of asking a genie and having your wishes granted.

They even quoted the Bible, where at Matthew 7:7 it tells us, "Ask and you shall receive, seek and you shall find, knock and the door shall be answered." Notice, it doesn't say, "Ask and sit back and wait because we'll come and get you, take you by limo and carry you in the door."

No, you still have to seek and when you find the right door, you have to knock before the door is answered. The assurance is that if you ask, you will be guided so that when you seek, you will find and when you knock the door will be answered. Action is not an option. It's imperative.

Inspired literally means 'breathed upon' and suggests that the recipient of inspiration is 'in spirit', guided by a higher power, God, intuition, the Universe, to take some action. Having engaged the magic of Future Pull, you will be guided by the Universe to move accurately toward the dream that you have created up ahead. You will be inspired. The guidance might come in the form of great ideas, synchronicity and serendipity, helpful strangers, or unexpected blessings. Your role is to watch for, accept and act on the guidance you receive.

As you stay alert and open to signs from the Universe, I know that you'll be constantly amazed at the strange twists and turns that lead you to your goal.

In 2005, Steve Jobs, CEO of Apple, gave a commencement speech at Stanford University that is often quoted. In that speech, talking about his career and how seemingly useless and random incidents and decisions all became part of the bigger picture in retrospect, he said,

> "You can't connect the dots looking forward; you can only connect them looking backwards. So you have to trust that the dots will somehow connect in your future. You have to trust in something—your gut, destiny, life, karma, whatever. This approach has never let me down, and it has made all the difference in my life."

Time to feel the Future Pull and start walking the path toward your dream. Can you see it? It's right up ahead. Just start walking.

Take a Lesson from the Inch Worm

You can eat an elephant, if you do it one bite at a time.
-Robert Riley

Now you have an amazing inspiring vision of the life you were meant to live. You have engaged the magic of the Universe and your future is pulling you towards your ideal life. You've looked at your present reality and considered what to take with you into the future and what to leave behind. You've made a list of 100 goals and set some very specific intentions of what you'd like to accomplish in the next few months. You've created some tools and a daily practice to keep you focused.

Are you ready for the journey? Are you ready to take action? Do you have any lingering fears or doubts that need to be dealt with? Are they real problems that might compromise your ability to take the actions you need to take to achieve your goals? Do you have to deal with them before you can step out confidently toward your future?

Or are they just boogeymen, monsters in the closet that will disappear as soon as you turn the light on or as soon as morning comes? Are they just irrational thoughts and imaginary hurdles that are holding you back?

It's too easy to put things off, waiting until absolutely everything is perfect. Everything will never be perfect. Don't let paralysis by analysis set in. Don't wait to get your 'ducks in a row' before taking action. Don't wait till the time is right, till you lose weight, save money, retire, move....the list of possible excuses is endless. Sometimes you just have to take a leap and trust that the Universe will provide you with wings.

The bucket list you've created contains one hundred things you'd like to have, do or be. That's a lot and it might be overwhelming. But I hope you've also identified several goals that you'd like to work on right now. A list of perhaps five things would be a great start.

Your immediate goals might be small things like using your fine china for everday meals (a great goal by the way, because you are certainly worthy of the very best). That's a fairly simple goal. You decide you want to do it and you do it. Okay, perhaps there are a few details to be worked out, like getting it out of storage, washing it, making room for it in the kitchen cupboards, having a yard sale to get rid of the current every day dishes, buying new napkins and placemats to go with it, and oh yeah, definitely new cutlery.

Suddenly, using your fine china seems like a much bigger goal, doesn't it? Really, some things don't have to become gigantic multi-year projects. Some things are 'just do it' goals. Just get out the china and start using it. Get rid of the old stuff, buy new napkins and cutlery when it seems right. Make a decision and act on it. You must have one or two goals that you can do RIGHT NOW! Right this minute. Put this book down and go do one of them! Right now! I'll wait!

....Pause....

You're back. Congratulations! You've accomplished one of your 100 goals. Did you cross it off your list and congratulate yourself? No? Well go do it now. I like to use bright colored highlighters just because it makes me happy to see all the bright colors as I cross them off. So go and cross it off your list and give yourself a big hug for getting it done. Go on! I'll wait!

....Pause....

Some goals really can be that easy. Some goals are easy but require persistence. You can't really cross a goal like that off your list until you've done it on a fairly consistent basis and it has become part of your life. For example, in your Ideal Day you may have had a ritual of sitting down with a cup of tea, quiet music playing and reading for an hour before bed. You may have included that evening routine in your list of 100 goals. One evening of doing that does not warrant crossing it off your list. But if you do it fairly consistently, perhaps four out of seven nights for a month, so that it feels like an important part of your routine, then you would probably feel justified in taking a nice bright pink highlighter and crossing it off your list.

Do you have any goals like that? Which one could you start making part of your life today? You don't have to do them all at once. Just start with one and do it consistently until it becomes a habit and you'd feel like something was missing if you skipped a day. Then cross it off your list and choose another.

Then there are the BIG goals – the ones that truly are gigantic. You might want to buy an RV and travel across the country. You might want to write a book. You might want to learn to play the guitar. You can't do those in a day, a week, or even a month. They are goals that have to be planned, have steps, have decisions to be made, money to be spent, people to connect with. They are the goals that can overwhelm you and make you want to go lay on the couch and watch reality tv.

That's when you need to become an inch worm. I think I have inch worms in my garden right now. I know they are destructive pests and I should probably be unhappy that I've seen a few of the tiny beasts sitting on my patio table. But you have to admit, they are kind of cute – so tiny and such a pretty bright green color. They just look so focused and methodical as they inch across my table. Inch by inch, not trying to take big leaps, just moving in a slow, measured way, getting where they are going no matter how long it takes.

Inch worms are really part of the 'Geometrid' family which means "earth-measurer" in Greek and are so named because it looks like they are measuring the ground, an inch at a time. We can take a lesson from the inch worm and take a slow measured approach to accomplishing our big goals.

I understand the debilitating effects of overwhelm. As a person who struggles with my own procrastination and perfectionism demons, I can become paralyzed by overwhelm. As an extremely creative 'idea' person I have lots of great ideas but many of those ideas are BIG ones and after a joyful period of daydreaming about all the possibilities, I end up mired in 'what next'. Then before you know it, my energy level hits bottom and I totally waste a few days before moving on to the next bright idea.

Making lists of things to do, steps to take towards my goals are a help, but those steps always tend to be fairly big in themselves. So for example, if I wanted to paint a large abstract painting that I could actually hang on my wall—a very real goal that now I'm so happy to say I've accomplished—I would have steps like a) buy canvas and paints, b) buy an easel, c) draw a picture, d) paint the picture, e) get it framed, f) hang it.

Then, if I really had no idea about what kind of canvas or paints I needed, I'd be bogged down in the very first step. So I'd rewrite my list and add a new first few steps: a) learn how to paint, b) measure the wall to see what size canvas I needed. You can see that as I added steps, they would lead to even more steps and before you knew it I'd be watching the Survivor rerun marathon on television.

Then I found SARK. SARK is fun, inspiring and realistic. SARK writes books that are produced in brightly colored, happy handwritten style full of drawings and stars and squiggles. They are perfect books for someone like me who's a bit ADD and very easily distracted.

They are also full of great ideas. One of her ideas is to take micro-movements, little tiny baby steps towards your goals. Ideally, you would want your micro-movements to be small enough so that you could complete them in twenty minutes.

Adapting the micro-movements idea, I could now come up with non-scary steps towards my goals. Now my list of steps I could complete towards my goal of painting a great big abstract might look like this: a) find the name of a painting store in the phone book; b) make a list of what I want to ask, c) call the store and ask if they know of painting classes, d) if they say yes and I like the sound of it, sign up for the class, e) if they say no or it doesn't sound like what I'm looking for, start over with a) and try another store.

Deanna Lohnes is a great example of someone who believes in the value of taking micro-movements. She keeps her list on her night stand and looks at it first thing in the morning. However, the real secret to Deanna's progress toward her goals is that she takes small steps on a daily basis. Deanna says she can get a lot accomplished as she rides the train to work every day. She reads her list of goals and decides on a small action that she can take right there on the spot if she can. Deanna used this micro-movement technique to write her book, *Footwork*. Appropriately, *Footwork* is about how people get stuck in wishful thinking, forgetting that they need to actually take action to achieve their dreams.

Because I'm a very visual person, I like to use mind maps. Mind maps are a free flowing way of recording the results of your brainstorming. Brainstorming is when you just try to think of as many ideas or steps as you can, in no particular order and without editing for quality. You just get it all down on paper. You don't have to be orderly, just scribble down as fast as you can all over the page.

Big pages are best for this, bristol board, large sketchbooks or even a blackboard. I have one whole wall in my home office painted with blackboard paint so that I can brainstorm in a really big way. After you've got it all out, everything you can think of, all over the paper, you start to make connections. First, circle the things that seem to be key steps. Then link the ideas or steps to the main step that they relate to by drawing lines connecting them.

My mind maps are always large and full of ideas, thoughts, questions and steps that I'd have to take to fulfill my goal.

After I have created a mind map, I can choose the first few steps, turn them into micro-movements and schedule them. That's key—actually making a schedule to carry out those micro-movements. The first step, looking in the yellow pages for a paint store that offers classes, might be something I could do right away to get me moving.

Don't use planning as a reason to put off getting started. Just decide on the first short list of micro-movements, choose one, and take action now! Before you know it, you'll be like the inchworm moving inch by inch toward the realization of your goals.

But continuous action is important. Taking tiny little baby steps will only get you where you're going if you take lots of them, one tiny little baby step after another. So set a goal for yourself of doing at least one thing every single day.

Some of your goals might not be the kind of things that have separate discrete steps that lend themselves to taking one step at a time. Some goals require just hard slogging work, day after day.

For example, writing a book. Some parts of writing can be turned into steps, like going to the library to do research, making an outline, choosing a layout, buying The Writers Market and finding potential publishers, or writing a book proposal. But at some point, you have to just start writing. And then you have to write, and write, and write, and write some more.

With goals like that, set a minimum time limit for working on your goal every single day. If you decide that you're going to write for fifteen minutes every single day, and do, you are much further along that if you decide that you're going to write for two hours on Sunday and then get distracted and don't write at all.

The difference between people who are successful in achieving their goals and those who aren't is sometimes just showing up. Just show up and do what you have committed to do. Even if you do nothing but write the same word over and over, or just empty your brain onto the page with no direction or plan, show up and do your time!

So what can you do right now, today, that will bring you closer to achieving your dreams? Whatever you think is stopping you is almost certainly a figment of your imagination.

Serendipity and Synchronicity

There is no such thing as chance; and what seems to us merest accident springs from the deepest source of destiny.
-Friedrich Schiller

    Serendipity and synchronicity! What musical words! They sound like smiles and laughter and dancing and poetry.

    Serendip was one of the ancient names for Sri Lanka and the word serendipity was coined by the 18th century English author, Horace Walpole. The word was actually based on the title of an old fairy tale called *The Three Princes of Serendip*. In one of his essays, Walpole referred to the story and said that, "as their highnesses traveled, they were always making discoveries, by accidents and sagacity, of things which they were not in quest of...."

Synchronicity is when events that are unrelated appear together in a meaningful way. Synchronicity, a meaningful confluence of events that appear to be unrelated, and serendipity, unexpected happy accidents and discoveries, are two of the ways that you'll know that the Universe is working to bring the life you dream of into your life. They are like signposts on the road to your future, guiding you as you make decisions about which way to turn, which path to take. The Universe will erect the signposts but it's your responsibility to look for them, pay attention to them and follow their clues.

When you have a chance meeting with someone you haven't seen in years and they tell you about a book to read that turns out to be exactly what you need at that moment, you've been touched by serendipity. If a piece of paper blows against your leg on a windy day and it turns out to be an invitation to an audition just when you've decided that you'd like to try acting, it most definitely is a sign from the Universe. You just never know when and how the Universe will send you a message, but you can be sure that if you've put out a call—sent out a visual prayer or a clear intention—somehow, someway, someday, the Universe will answer.

    We are bombarded with people, noise, information and opportunities. It's very much like driving along a busy highway feeling almost assaulted by billboards, neon signs, and moving digital displays. How do you figure out which ones are signs and which ones are just 'urban blight'? How do you screen out the extraneous so that you can hone in on the important? You have a built in automatic universal positioning system. You just have to fine tune it and keep it turned on.

    Your vision board and Ideal Day exercise are components of that automatic universal positioning system. They act as a filter, helping you to identify and focus on those things that are in line with your larger goals. It isn't really a conscious process, but rather acts at a deeper level. You'll find that, even though perhaps you haven't looked at your vision board or read your Ideal Day recently, you've made choices that have pulled you closer to the future that you've envisioned. Imagine how much clearer your future will appear and how much easier it will be to navigate the many possible routes to reach it, if you make reviewing your vision board and Ideal Day a daily practice.

Even if your universal positioning system is tuned to the right frequency, the message can still be distorted. Just like when you're listening to the radio, too much static will make it impossible to discern what the message really is. All you'll hear is noise. Static that interferes with your ability to tune in to the frequency of the Universe could be caused by many things—distractions, negative thoughts, clutter, mental junk food. Taking time to be quiet and connect with your deeper self, the Universe within you, will help to reduce the static and allow you to tune in and receive your clues from the Universe more clearly.

So what will it sound like when the Universe sends you a message, 'go this way', or 'that's the wrong way, don't go there'? Often, it's a gut feeling or what we call intuition. A 'follow this star' feeling might be excitement, happiness, joy, heightened interest, or just a calm and quiet assurance that this is the right thing to do. A 'wrong way' sign is perhaps a gut feeling that something isn't quite right, a suspicion that something is too good to be true, a hesitation.

On occasion I've ignored those warning signs to my own detriment. I have sometimes talked myself out of them because I have tried to give people the benefit of the doubt when I have a suspicion that they aren't quite who they say they are. The Bible says, in 2 Corinthians 11:14 that, "even Satan disguises himself as an angel of light."

Now I don't believe in Satan but I think that verse is still a good warning that sometimes tempting things are not good for us. Look at cake! Looks great! Tastes great! Not good! It's much more likely that you'll misjudge whether something is good for you when you override your inner guidance system with what you think is rational thought.

Your soul, the deep quiet part of you that is connected to everything else in the Universe knows what is right and wrong, what is good and bad and what is safe and not safe. Listen to it. Spend time each day connecting and checking in.

When you are in receipt of a sign from the Universe, you can often tell whether it's right for you or not by whether it causes you to expand or contract. Expansion, that feeling of your chest opening up, will only happen when it's safe for you to do so. If the Universe, your inner guidance system, detects danger, it will cause contraction and you'll feel a sense of constriction or closing up in your chest as you pull in to protect yourself.

You have many senses besides the usual touch, sight, scent, and hearing and your energy field will contract when your body receives a sign that you may be in danger. I saw this happen when I was learning to be a feng shui practitioner. As I mentioned, I had not yet freed myself of my rigid religious beliefs and so when we learned to use a pendulum I was very resistant. Everyone else's pendulum was swinging freely and mine hung straight and motionless.

At one point, because I was completely unable to make anything happen, I was asked to act as an observer.

One person sat blindfolded on a chair in the middle of the room. Everyone else, or at least everyone else who was able to sense energy, stood around the perimeter of the room and then, with their eyes closed, moved in towards the person in the centre until they sensed the edge of her energy field, where they stopped. They all stopped about five or six feet from the seated person. Then the instructor quietly took a kitchen knife out of a bag and very gently and slowly moved it towards the blindfolded person's back, stopping about six inches away and returning the knife to the paper bag.

All the energy sensors still had their eyes closed and so did not see what she was doing. They were then instructed to again move to the edge of the seated person's energy field. Surprisingly, now they were able to move in to approximately a foot from her. Her energy field had shrunk dramatically. It had contracted in response to the threat of the knife even though neither she nor any of the ring of people had seen what the instructor had in the bag.

It was an interesting lesson on how our bodies stay attuned to everything that is going on around us. We are intimately connected to everything and everyone around us and our spidey senses are tuned in even though we may not be aware of it. Getting in touch with your inner self will allow you to take accurate readings and act on the energy that is affecting you.

Back when my dream was to own a home, a whole series of events and chance meetings led ultimately to the purchase of the house I now own. First of all, on the morning before New Years Day, my son and I went for breakfast. There I met a man, Mike, who had been in one of my early life skills programs. Mike had a beautiful German shepherd and in the process of greeting him and catching up on the years since I had last seen him, I asked how the dog was. He said she had just had puppies and asked me if I would like one. As I have mentioned, I was living in a housing cooperative where the pet limit was eight legs maximum so I said, "Oh I wish I could but I already have two cats."

My son said, "Come on, mum, you need to move out of there anyway. You've always wanted a German shepherd." He then told Mike to bring his dogs over for me to choose one. I objected but both John and Mike overruled me.

An hour later, Mike was at my door with the two most beautiful little German shepherd puppies. One of them immediately chose me and so I was the owner of the dog of my Ideal Day.

That night, at a New Years Eve party, I was talking to someone about needing to buy a house and telling them that I was pretty sure I'd never be approved for a mortgage. Someone that I barely knew overheard me and told me to try his investment company because he had felt the same way but was approved and, in fact, received a lower mortgage rate because he became a client.

I followed up and received a pre-approved mortgage. When I went back to work after the holidays, I told a friend what I had done, that I now had a dog and I was looking for a house. She said her daughter had a friend who was pregnant and they were thinking of selling their little house and buying a larger one. That night she called me and said she had spoken to them and I could go and see it if I wanted, even though it wasn't on the market. Well, it was perfect and it had a very large fully fenced yard, perfect for my dog, Ruby. Within days we had come to an agreement and I was the proud owner of my very first home.

From start to finish it was a symphony of serendipity and synchronicity and it rolled out effortlessly. That's another sign of when the Universe is showing you the way; it will be seamless and feel like it was meant to happen.

If the road is fraught with problems, it is often a sign that it's the wrong road. For example, after I had grown my business and won several government contracts, I went from a sole owner, home based business to a small business with twelve staff. At one point we were looking for a new location and the one I had my heart set on was suddenly rented to someone else and I lost out. I was disappointed and grumpy.

I remember one of the staff, Shantelle, said in a cheery, extremely irritating way, "Well that's okay. It just means there's something better right around the corner." You know, sometimes it doesn't matter whether that's true or whether it's just what you would normally believe in, at that moment I was just plain grouchy and unappreciative of her optimism. In fact I was kind of snarly. But she was right. A few days later we heard about another possibility that was less expensive, a storefront on a main street that would be much more visible. The road to renting that location was smooth and trouble-free. A sure sign it was the right choice.

We are not privy to the workings of the Universe and sometimes have to trust that it is all unfolding as it should. If you believe that the Universe is beneficent and bountiful, it is a lot easier to trust that all will work out. I have had much evidence that I am blessed and protected by the Universe so I find it, usually, easy to believe that things are working or will work out in my favour.

Sometimes, for example, I have a day where everything is going wrong. You know the kind of day I am talking about. I'm running late, slept in, can't find my keys and then perhaps run into construction that forces me to change my usual route. I can take those delays calmly because I believe that, even though I may not always know why, it is probably better for me to follow my instincts than to push through no matter what. I know that if I stay relaxed and follow the signs, it will be better for me in the end. It always is.

Oh sure, I also have days when it appears everything is going wrong and I'm not so relaxed about it. When I get stressed and start to make it all about me, that's when I end up in a bad place. That's when I lose my connection to the Universe and when I start to make bad choices. That's when I need to step back, refocus on what's important and what isn't, and then go with the flow. No use swimming upstream when you can float downstream so much more easily.

If it seems like a struggle, then you are probably fighting the flow of the Universe. A friend described it this way, "It's like the difference between getting on a plane and letting it fly you to your destination and strapping a plane on your back and flapping your arms wildly."

If you have clearly set an intention and created the future you were meant to live, then it will pull you effortlessly towards it. You just need to let go, watch for the signs, and follow them.

Boost the Power of Future Pull

Choose always the way that seems the best, however rough it may be. Custom will soon render it easy and agreeable.
                                                              -Pythagoras

You're taking inspired action, watching for the signposts and following the clues. In spite of your best efforts, you might on occasion find that you start to slow down and even begin to doubt that you're on the right track. You may find that your energy lags. You start to lose focus and get lost in the day to day detritus of your nowadays life. You begin to forget that you have a life waiting for you up ahead. Your future loses the power to pull you.

It happens to all of us. We all have different challenges to deal with. Mine is that I am an 'idea person'. I am easily distracted by bright shiny objects, fresh new ideas, exciting possibilities. The world is so full of wonderful things and thoughts that I can easily lose focus and head off in another direction. Then something else calls to me and I make another turn and before you know it I'm completely lost and wondering where I'm going and why.

If I want to reach the life I've created up ahead, I have to stay focused on my vision and let it pull me towards it. That means that sometimes I have to stop, get rid of distractions, refocus and head out again on the right path.

You may have other challenges that pull you off track. You may be dealing with an inner doubter or limiting beliefs that try to convince you that you can't achieve your goals. Or outer doubters, like partners, parents, employers or friends who feel that they should 'warn' you against what they see as the folly of being unrealistic.

You might be facing some very real issues around basic survival, such as money, employment, relationships or health. In some cases, it is easy to become overwhelmed with real life concerns and it would be unethical and unrealistic of me to imply that you should ignore them all and just move on blindly towards your goals. If you have to take a job right now to pay the rent, even though it isn't the job of your dreams, then absolutely you have to do that. If you are faced with a life threatening illness, it would be silly to try to ignore it away. In situations like these, you need to decide the best action for you to take right now, deal with it and resolve it. Then you can refocus and step out again on our path towards your ideal life.

When you get temporarily sidelined while you deal with life issues, your biggest challenge will be not losing hope, not letting doubt and hopelessness take over. When you have to take a brief detour, stay focused on the big picture. Keep that clear compelling vision of your future front and centre so that as the way clears, and it will, you can get back on the path.

Remember that this might be an unexpected turn that will take you closer to your Ideal Day. You often can't connect the dots and see that everything worked out perfectly until later. Sometimes it's when you feel most lost that you must just keep walking, keeping a clear vision of your goal, and trusting that the Universe is on your side.

You don't have control over some things in your day to day life, but you do have absolute control over your attitude and the thoughts you choose to think.

Even when you are faced with seemingly insurmountable problems, that you think you have no control over, you have far more control than you may think. You have control over the most important thing of all. You can choose how you respond. Never think you have no choice. You always choose how the attitude you will take and the thoughts you will think.

Your attitude and thoughts have a remarkable impact on reality and so, ultimately, by choosing your thoughts, you choose your reality.

When you feel like you are getting sidelined, ask yourself a few focused questions:

>Is this a real detour, or is it a mirage?
>
>Am I just being fooled by fear and doubt into believing that I have to give up my dream?
>
>What is the risk of staying focused on my goals?
>
>What is the worst that could happen if I reject this distraction and stay focused?
>
>What is the risk of putting my dream on the backburner? Am I willing to take that risk?
>
>What decision am I being called on right now to make and what are my options?

Take a short, medium and long view of the situation. Get clear about the decision that you need to make, make it and then act on it.

A decision is not a vague thing; not a maybe thing. A decision means that you make a choice and cut off any other option or any doubt about the direction in which you must travel. Perhaps that is the quality of decision making that makes it so difficult—the feeling that once made, you cannot change your mind. When you decide on a course of action, you must start to act on it. You cannot say you've made a decision and then continue to consider other options. If you do that, then you haven't made a decision.

One of the challenges in making a decision is that you begin to see it as a right or wrong situation. You start to believe that there is one right choice and that any other choice is wrong. As a result, you become paralyzed with fear that you will make the wrong choice. When that happens, you abdicate your right and responsibility to choose your direction and you lose energy and motivation. You grind to a stop.

In her book, *Feel the Fear and Do It Anyway*, Susan Jeffers presents a no-fear decision making technique. This technique, when I've used it in career coaching, has been of great value in reducing paralysis by analysis.

It's very simple. Take a sheet of paper and draw several lines vertically from the top to the bottom of the page so that you have a series of columns.

At the top of each column write a label to describe one of your options. You should have one column for each of your options. Then below each of your choices, list all of the things that are good about that choice. Don't worry about the negatives of each choice, just the positive.

Repeat the process for every option you can think of. When you've exhausted all your options and all the benefits of each choice, count up how many positives you have in each column. Almost always, you'll have one column where the benefits outnumber all the other columns. That is the option to choose.

This technique takes the focus off of the negative possibilities. It is a reminder that you don't know what is just around the corner and that, based on what you know right now, most likely each of the options has some good in it. You can just choose the one that seems, right now, knowing what you know, to be the best out of a selection of good possibilities.

I always have to remind my career coaching clients about this. Often, people will try to make career decisions based on their perception of whether a potential employer is well established and therefore can offer stability. In reality, there could be many things impacting the viability of a company or the size of their workforce. Some you may be able to predict. For example, if the product a certain company manufactures is becoming obsolete, they have to adjust or shut down. How they adjust or the actions they take to deal with the change in consumer demand, however, will most likely be unknown to you. You have to make the best decision you can at that time, with the resources you have available and the knowledge that you have.

After you've considered all of the possibilities and selected the one that has the most benefits, consider it from another perspective. Ask yourself these questions:

> What will be the impact of my decision tomorrow?
>
> What will be the impact of my decision next week?
>
> What might be the impact of my decision next month?
>
> What will be the impact of my decision next year?
>
> What will be the impact of my decision in ten years?

When you ask yourself these questions, remember that you do not have the same perspective as the Universe. In fact, your view is pretty limited really. You don't know what will happen next week, next month or even in the next five minutes. So, in spite of your best efforts to consider every possible outcome, you can only make the best decision now based on what you know right now. Then rely on the beneficence of the Universe and the power of Future Pull to roll everything out just the way it should.

Of course, sometimes you might lose your way just because, like me, you've become distracted. Then you need to go back and review the work you did when you were developing your compelling vision. Read your Ideal Day, take a long look at your vision board, go back to visualizing every day, reset your intentions and affirmations. Recheck your goals and celebrate your progress.

Sometimes you just need to revive the excitement. Think of how a sailboat has to continually adjust the sails and change direction to catch the wind. You may have to do the same. Scan your environment, adjust and adapt. If you are slowing down you may need to refocus on your vision and make small revisions in your plan.

Is there something you can do right now to take a little leap toward your vision? Try it and feel the power of Future Pull pick up again.

Chart Your Course

Journal writing is a voyage to the interior.
-Christina Baldwin

As you move along your life path toward the life of your dreams, it can be easy to lose track of your progress. You might start to feel that you're just spinning your wheels and not getting anywhere. Keeping a journal is a great way to record your advancement and to remind yourself of where you were when you started this journey and how much you've advanced toward your goals.

In early 2006, I was at a very, very low point in my life. For four years I had been dealing with many issues and over the last year in particular, I was dealing with financial, emotional and health issues. I was deeply depressed and just couldn't see any relief in sight. I remember just before Christmas of 2005, I heard a song by the Cranberries that had a chorus that went something like, "Let me make it through December. I promise I'll remember." That became my theme song. To me it was about carrying on and learning from the mistakes that brought me to such a low point.

On January 30, 2006, I was getting ready for work with the television on in the background. I heard an elderly man being interviewed about surviving cancer. It caught my attention and I sat down and listened for a while. He was telling the interviewer that when he was diagnosed, twenty-two years ago, he had made a conscious decision. He said he could choose to live or to die and he chose to live to see his grandchildren grow.

I thought, "Twenty-two years from now I'll be seventy-seven. Just like him. Do I want to be a happy vibrant seventy-seven year old like him? Or do I want to spend the next twenty-two years feeling like this?" I decided I wanted to be happy.

I went and found a journal that I had abandoned back in 1999. I was always starting and stopping journals. And I started writing. That morning, this is what I wrote:

> "A long time since my last entry in this journal. I see 1999 was a good year. Has EVERYTHING gone downhill from there? I'm in a low place – so low that I feel like my life is over or that I wish it would be – soon. I feel old and hopeless. My dreams, I had so many of them, and they just seem like a joke now. I feel too old and worn out."

It hurts even to read that and remember how sad and worn out I felt. I wrote pages that morning, laying out what I saw as all my mistakes and failures that had brought me to such a low place. Then I went to work. On February 3rd, I wrote:

> "I see a light! Could it be daylight? Could it mean I see a way out? Maybe!"

On February 11th, I wrote:

> "What a difference a week makes! So much has happened in the past week. I have a new job, a much better one with more money. I went out with friends last night and I'm feeling much more happy and optimistic."

My life turned around 180 degrees in less than two weeks. Was it the journaling? I don't think so but the journal recorded the turnaround and when I go back and read it, it reminds me that things can change in a heartbeat. It reminds me of how sad and low I was, how I had virtually given up, and how quickly I regained my optimism and a level of happiness that I hadn't felt in a very long time.

Ever since that January 30th morning, I have continued to journal. Every now and then I go back through my journals and check out what I was doing on the same day last year, or the year before. I like to see how much I've progressed.

I also find that I am learning from my experiences, both good and bad, more effectively because I can see the commonalities. When I make the same mistake several times and have the same results, I can actually see it there in writing. I'm not so likely to forget it and make the same mistake over and over and over.

But by far, the most pleasure I get from reading past journals is from celebrating how far I've come since that very low winter of 2005. If I start to take things for granted or start to feel that I'm not making any progress, all I need to do is go back and read an old journal and I can see that I have made tremendous progress.

Keeping a journal will help you to recognize and celebrate as you see your journey to your ideal life unfold. You can write in it every day or just a few times a week. At a minimum I write in it every Sunday morning as I have breakfast and coffee on my deck. Don't let it become just a list of everything you've done over the day or week. Pour out your feelings and fears as well. Then you'll be able to see even more clearly how you change as you advance towards your dream life.

For me, journaling has become a valued ritual. I like to buy large black coil bound art journals. They are big and lie flat. They have no lines and so I am free to write as big and loopy as I want, to draw if I want, and to paste in pictures or news articles. Every new year, I like to buy a collection of gel pens in different colors so that I can choose a color that reflects my mood.

Sunday mornings, I make my omelette and a coffee, take my journal and the chosen pen, and a random selection of older journals to peruse, and I head outside to my deck. I eat breakfast slowly and then record the day, the weather, my mood and all the 'stuff' that is resting at the top of my mind. After that I usually read the last entry and update anything that might have been mentioned in there.

Without fail, when I have completed my journaling ritual I feel optimistic and ready to start my day. Sometimes I make a list of what I want to do and then I close it and start to take action.

Journaling is just one of the tools that will help keep you on track and record your triumphs and progress, but I believe it is an important one and I hope you will give it a try.

Allow the Universe to Unfold

If you lose hope, somehow you lose the vitality that keeps life moving, you lose that courage to be, that quality that helps you go on in spite of it all. And so today, I still have a dream.
-Martin Luther King Jr.

Allow the Universe to Unfold

To accomplish great things, we must not only act, but also dream; not only plan but also believe.
                                        -Anatole France

You have created a compelling vision and you are taking inspired action. The next step, for many of us, is perhaps the hardest of all. Now you have to allow the Universe to unfold.

You have to give up control. You have to quit worrying. You have to carry on, believing in your vision and taking one step after another even when it appears that nothing is happening.

Allowing is key to the concept of Future Pull. To access the power of Future Pull, you create such a compelling vision of your ideal life that it becomes a reality waiting for you up ahead. It's like the Emerald City sitting at the end of the Yellow Brick Road. All you need to do is set out on the path, take one step after another, and follow the signposts.

Future Pull will lay the road out for you, one yellow brick at a time. You just walk it, trusting that it's leading you towards the future that you envisioned.

Let Go of the How's and When's

*Trying creates impossibilities;
letting go creates what is desired.*
　　　　　　　　-Stalking Wolf, Apache Elder

If you were brought up to believe in the power of hard work, allowing the Universe to unfold can appear to be the very opposite of what you were taught.

Allowing can feel wimpy or passive. The urge will be to plan the how's and when's of achieving your dreams, set objectives and timelines for achievement, and cross items off your to-do list. Planning and scheduling and working hard to achieve your goals feels like you are accomplishing something, even if you aren't seeing the results you expect. At least for a while. Then you start to feel like 'what's the use' and you lose momentum. At some point you might even feel like giving up and declaring, "What a load of bunk! That stuff doesn't work!"

Allowing the Universe to unfold as it will requires trust and patience; often hard to come by qualities. In our current environment, we expect action and we expect it NOW. The days of sending a letter and waiting weeks for a response are over. Now we send an email and expect a response within minutes, or we send another. When we call someone on the telephone, we no longer want to leave a voicemail. We want to have a variety of numbers—land line, cell phone, Skype—and we try all of them until we get a response. You've sent your request to the Universe and you want what you want, and you want it NOW.

The Universe doesn't operate on your timeline. The response from the Universe will appear in good time. Good time is a good way to view it because the

Universe has a larger, more all encompassing view and understands when the time is right. The Universe won't be pushed into responding on your timeline.

Allowing is about understanding that you are a co-creator of your reality. You are working with the Universe, doing your part but then trusting and knowing that the Universe will come through for you.

Mike Dooley, one of the teachers on *The Secret* and the visionary behind www.tut.com, likens it to playing ball with the Universe. You throw out the ball...then what? Do you race over, catch it and throw it back to yourself? Of course not! You throw the ball and trust that the other person, in this case the Universe, will catch it and toss it back.

The Universe will come through. All you have to do is relinquish the need to control and allow the Universe to do its work in its own way and in its own time. With our limited vision, we may not be able to fathom or predict how things will work out and sometimes it may seem like everything is going off track. Allowing is recognizing that we may not be able to plan and see the circuitous route that the Universe is taking. The Universe will send us signs and our job is to continue to move steadily in the direction that we are being shown.

Does that sound a bit like relying on luck or fate? It's neither. Relying on fate or luck would be sitting back and saying, 'Well I guess it's just not meant to be", and giving up. Some people confuse that type of thinking with Allowing but it's far different. If you believe in fate or luck, you are giving up all involvement in the process of co-creating your life. You are making the Universe, or in this case, luck or fate, solely responsible for everything that happens in your life. Nothing could be further from the truth.

You are a key player in creating the life you desire. You have created your vision; decided exactly who you want to be, what you want to have, and what opportunities or events you want to have happen in your life. You've asked for it, and you are taking steps towards the life you have asked for. However, sometimes things happen in ways that we can't predict. Synchronicity and serendipity happen and bring us closer to our vision in unexpected ways. You cannot predict or control the Universe but you can pay attention and you can choose how you respond when you have an unexpected turn of events.

People call Colleen McGunnigle, a Long Island graphic artist and book designer, the 'manifesting queen' because she seems to effortlessly attract business and trips into her life. In spite of appearances, Colleen recognizes that Allowing is the aspect of life creation where it is all too easy to get hung up.

A strong believer in visualization, Colleen will create a picture of her future as clearly and specifically as she can. She is careful, however, not to invest in the details. Colleen uses them to get into it, engage her senses, and feel the joy of living in her dream, but then she releases them while maintaining the substance of the vision. She pictures herself holding her dream and then spreads her hands and releases it to the universe.

Colleen knows that desperation and neediness can create barriers to her manifestation. She says it's like trying to drive with her foot on the brake; when her ego gets involved, it shuts off her connection with the Universe and puts a stop to her manifestation power. Instead she holds a lightness and feeling of playing with the Universe.

When negativity starts to seep into Colleen's mind, she does stream of consciousness writing, pouring all of the 'I can't do it' thoughts onto paper. She reads it over and underlines all of the words and phrases that are charged with negativity and then turns them around, choosing more Allowing and positive ways to express herself.

Remember, there is reality and then there is our own interpretation of reality. Things are as they are. How we read them and react to them determines the outcome and, ultimately, our life.

Allowing and trusting that the Universe will come through is about letting situations, people, and things, be as they are. It means you don't judge them, try to fix them or change them. It doesn't mean taking a victim role or giving up. Allowing has power. It's not a victim role. Allowing is choosing to allow others or situations to be as they are and then choosing how you will respond. Will you be open to others, to ideas, to possibilities? Are you ready to allow the Universe to unfold? Will you allow transformation?

Give Up the Need to Know

The best thing about the future is that it comes only one day at a time.
-Abraham Lincoln

When you create a vision for your future and enable Future Pull, you are trusting that the Universe will come through and do its part to help you get there. Now if the Universe emailed you a nice neat document with a plan for exactly how it was going to bring that about, you wouldn't be taken by surprise by any of the twists and turns on the path. Unfortunately, or perhaps fortunately, that's not the way it works.

In reality, you have no idea what is going to happen next year, next week, tomorrow, or even in the next five minutes. What does happen may have unforeseen consequences that affect how your plans unfold. It may be the catalyst that brings your future, exactly as you visualized it, right to you in a rush of unexpected happenings. Or it may be a little more convoluted than that and you may be called on to summon up vast amounts of patience and trust.

But always keep in mind that you don't know everything and everything and anything can change at any time.

I know that it's easy to become almost paralyzed with indecision when faced with such unknowns. That's when allowing the Universe to unfold comes in. Keep your vision clear and focused. If you have to choose a path, choose it based on your bigger vision, paying attention to the signposts and your inner knowing. Don't start switching trains in mid-journey just because you start to have doubt based on what might happen.

On the other hand, you need a level of flexibility in your goals and plans. Your goals and plans were created based on information you had at the time you created them. That information may have changed and you may need to adjust. But don't give up on your vision just because the nice neat plan that you developed has been side-tracked.

Your vision is still working for you. Keep your picture of the life you aspire to clear and strong. Maintain your daily practice of visualizing it clearly and sending a message to the Universe that your intention is still powerful. Most important of all, don't let doubt creep in and short circuit the power of Future Pull.

Energy Soup

We all take different paths in life, but no matter where we go, we all take a little of each other everywhere.
                                        -Unknown

We live in an energy soup. As part of the great Universe we are intimately connected to everything and everyone around us. That's why others can so profoundly affect our energy level, our mood, and our motivation and why we so profoundly affect others. What a great responsibility!

Have you ever shared your dreams with someone just to have them skewered by well-intended but deadly warnings to play it safe, give them up, don't rock the boat? I had a wonderful friend for many years. She has since passed on but for twenty years she was my very closest friend. She was one of the kindest, most loving people I've ever known but she was also a dream-killer. I would share with her my Ideal Day visions and she would tell me how I should change it to be more 'realistic'. A conversation with her about my hopes and dreams could leave me laying around and moping on the couch for days. Do you have a friend like that?

Since then, I've had to consider that perhaps I shared my dreams with her so that she could talk me out of them. Then I didn't have to follow through. I had a good reason— usually many of them—to give up. Surrounding yourself with dream-killers is just another, very subtle, form of self-sabotage.

Instead, surround yourself with people who will support you as you move towards the future you were born to live. Christina Kane, a singer/songwriter and coach who specializes in coaching programs for creative types, says you should surround yourself with 'Extreme Encouragers'.

Surround yourself with people who are living examples of the qualities you want to embody. Jack Canfield, the pre-eminent life success coach and author of *The Success Principles*, says that you become the average of the five people you spend the most time with. So make sure you spend time with people who are going to result in you becoming your very best self. Choose to share your energy with people who live 'bigger lives', take more risks, are open to the possibilities and look for the positives in any situation. Don't spend so much time with people who are 'psychic vampires', sucking your energy dry and shutting down your dreams. You'll know who they are by how you feel after you've spent time with them.

Choose to spend time with people who really listen. They let you joyfully talk about your dreams and plans and they really listen. They aren't just waiting for a break to jump in and tell you why 'it won't work'. They don't just use clichés. You know what I mean—someone who says, "That's nice", or "Oh

Jackie, another big idea, you're so creative." Sounds like a nice compliment on the surface, right? But you somehow feel like you've been treated like a puppy, patted on the head and told "You're so cute." You don't feel validated or empowered.

Encouraging, supportive people aren't vapid. They can acknowledge the scary stuff – making huge changes and taking life leaps can be very scary and it's okay to recognize that. But real encouragers know that only you know what is best for you and they give you credit for knowing that and making wise choices when the time is right. They know that life is full of twists and turns and that we can never predict what is just around the corner. Encouragers know and communicate their confidence that you will learn and grow to meet any challenges that are ahead.

Who are you sharing your dreams with? If you feel deflated and doubtful after spending time with a friend, perhaps you need to spend a little less time with that person. If you feel inspired, energized and positive about your future, then that is a person you can trust with your dreams.

Of course, energy doesn't flow in only one direction. Look at your own behaviour. Are you a downer? If you are, perhaps the very people you want in your life – the positive people who talk and walk their dreams – are avoiding you. Are you an encourager? If you start to behave as an Extreme Encourager, you will attract like-minded people and find that you are pulling people into your life who 'live big', see the possibilities, and support others in their dreams.

For a period of time I was in a job that I hated. I was bored. I didn't feel valued. I had a really negative attitude and I voiced it constantly. Then one day, for some reason, I had a turnaround. There was a blank whiteboard on the wall as you entered our office area and one day I thought, "That board is boring. It needs something on it." I wrote an inspiring quote on it and the next day I wrote another.

No one saw me do it for a few weeks and I could hear people talking about it and wondering who the 'Quote Fairy' was. Then one day, someone caught me writing my quote. People started sending me new ones to include. The whole atmosphere in the office was lightened, just by that simple change. But the most telling result for me was when two co-workers came in and asked me where Jackie was. I just looked at them puzzled. I was sitting right there! They said, "No the Jackie that was all doom and gloom. What did you do with her?"

Obviously my own bad attitude had really impacted the team and with just a change in my own thoughts and behaviour I contributed to a change in the energy in the whole office.

We affect people with more than just the message that we are communicating with our words. Our entire presence affects others – how we dress, our body language, how we behave, how we treat others. I'll give you an example that will show that not only does it affect others, it affects our own feelings and attitudes.

I was once leading a life skills program for women who were almost all girlfriends of gang members and they looked it. Not only did they dress in clothing that was representative of the subculture they were part of, but they behaved in the group as though they were in a bar or out on the street. They would literally jump up at the slightest provocation and start physically fighting. Those who were not part of that subculture and who were in the program because they really wanted to change their lives, were often intimidated and some of them withdrew from the group. It was not only exhausting for me but sometimes even scary.

I tried several things to improve the atmosphere. I developed a list of 'rules' such as no swearing, no fighting, and no coming to the group drunk. They not only rebelled against that list of 'rules', they actually went to the project manager and said I had threatened them. The energy soup that we were all swimming in was more like a toxic sewer. I had to do something.

The most surprising action I took, the one that had the most impact on the participants, was establishing a dress code. As part of the program, the women were given a small amount of money to purchase clothing appropriate for them to find employment. I arranged for them to get the money early and then made it a requirement that they had to wear those clothes to the group. What a change! As soon as they started dressing differently, they began to behave differently.

You may have found that yourself. Have you ever spent the day in your pyjamas, not showering, just plodding around in your slippers? Sounds cozy, but I can tell you from experience that if you are self-employed and work from home, and if you choose to work like that, in your pj's, your business is doomed. Your attitude and get up and go, will get up and go. Taking the time and energy to dress appropriately for your clients, even if they don't actually see you, demonstrates your commitment to them. Taking the time and energy to make yourself look the very best you can, also demonstrates your commitment to yourself. You deserve that as well.

Not only do you live in an energy soup, you are also an energy soup and you need to treat yourself with the care, love and attention that you want from others. Your opinion of yourself impacts you greatly. Be an Extreme Encourager to others, seek out Extreme Encouragers for yourself, but most importantly, be an Extreme Encourager to yourself.

Guard Your Thoughts

The pessimist sees difficulty in every opportunity. The optimist sees opportunity in every difficulty.
－Sir Winston Churchill

Being careful to surround yourself only with people who are positive, encouraging and supportive is important. But sometimes the worst culprit, the person we really have to watch out for, is living right inside of us. After all, I've never had anyone try to tie me down and force me to eat a full tub of ice cream but when I'm struggling with my own thoughts and my own cravings and desires, the effect is the same.

Emmet Fox, back in 1935, wrote *The Seven Day Mental Diet*. It is still in print today and it is widely available on the Internet.

In *The Seven Day Mental Diet*, Fox talks about The Great Cosmic Law in this way:

> "The most important of all factors in your life is the mental diet on which you live. It is the food which you furnish to your mind that determines the whole character of your life. It is the thoughts you allow yourself to think, the subjects that you allow your mind to dwell upon, which make you and your surroundings what they are. Everything in your life today, the state of your body, whether healthy or sick, the state of your fortune, whether prosperous or impoverished, the state of your home, whether happy or the reverse, the present condition of every phase of your life in fact is entirely conditioned by the thoughts and feelings which you have entertained in

the past, the habitual tone of your past thinking. And the conditions of your life tomorrow, and next week, and next year, will be entirely conditioned by the thoughts and feelings which you choose to entertain from now onwards."

There is another little book, a booklet really, called *You Can't Afford the Luxury of a Negative Thought—A Book for People with Any Life-Threatening Illness—Including Life.* Peter McWilliams, the author, admits he is a born pessimist. In fact, he describes his outlook this way,

"I come before you a certified expert on the subject: I'm a confirmed negaholic. I don't just see a glass that's half-full and call it half-empty; I see a glass that's completely full and worry that someone's going to tip it over."

McWilliams calls negative thinking a disease and outlines the three part cure:

> "(1) spend more time focusing on the positive things in your life (Accentuate the Positive);
>
> (2) spend less time thinking negatively (Eliminate the Negative); and
>
> (3) enjoy each and every moment you can (Latch on to the Affirmative)."

It's interesting that he talks about it in terms of a disease and cure. Emmet Fox does the same and he gives us a seven day prescription. It's a tough one.

> "This then is your prescription. For seven days you must not allow yourself to dwell for a single moment on any kind of negative thought. You must watch yourself for a whole week as a cat watches a mouse, and you must not under any pretence allow your mind to dwell on any thought that is not positive, kind, constructive, optimistic. This discipline will be so strenuous that you could

not maintain it consciously for much more than a week, but I do not ask you to do so. A week will be enough, because by that time the habit of positive thinking will begin to be established. Some extraordinary changes for the better will have come into your life, encouraging you enormously, and then the future will take care of itself. The new way of life will be so attractive and so much easier than the old way that you will find your mentality aligning itself almost automatically."

Are you up for the challenge? He admits the Seven Day Mental Diet is strenuous. You have to be vigilant. Not so much to stop negative thoughts from coming into your mind, because they will, like it or not. You have to be vigilant so that they don't start to roost in your mind, build nests and set up homes where they can live comfortably and act as barriers that prevent you from getting to your dreams.

Each time you become aware that you have been invaded by a negative thought, just let it go and turn your mind to a more positive thought. That's the key—turning your mind to another more positive thought. It is difficult to just stop thinking something. It is far more effective to begin thinking about a positive thought than to try to stop thinking about a negative thought.

Do you have habitual negative thoughts? Many of us have adopted as truth, hurtful and derogatory slurs that we heard in the past. If you were told over and over again as a child that you were bratty, too noisy, or wouldn't amount to much, you have probably continued to tell yourself the same thing as an adult. You don't even need to be around negative people, you're a cat-calling crowd all by yourself.

It might be helpful, if you know that you have habitual negative thoughts, to prepare for them by writing some better phrases that you can turn to. If you tell yourself that you always give up so why bother starting anything, write a more positive thought that you can adopt whenever that negative thinking slips in.

It's important that you make it the opposite of the thinking you want to erase and that it is believable. This process is called re-framing and here are a few examples of how re-framing might sound:

Negative thought:
"I'm such a loser. I never finish anything so I might as well give up now."

Positive thought:
"I have completed many projects successfully and I'm enjoying working on this exciting new idea."

Negative thought:
"Bruce hurt my feelings when he said that but he was right and probably other people think that too."

Positive thought:
"Bruce hurt my feelings when he said that and I will tell him and ask for an apology. I am worthy of respect and kindness and I do not choose to spend time with people who are hurtful or disrespectful."

Negative thought:

"People wouldn't be interested in my ideas so I'll just keep quiet at the meeting. I always get things wrong and make a fool of myself."

Positive thought:

"I have a great idea and I can't wait to bring it up at the meeting. I am ready to present it in an enthusiastic way and I'm sure people will want to get involved."

Notice the last example in particular. Remember when we talked about visualization and how what you think creates your reality? If you have a history of making suggestions that are shot down, perhaps your own attitude and belief about how your ideas will be accepted is attracting the very reaction that you dread. Try changing your thinking from negative to positive, follow it up with a strong visualization of how your wished-for outcome might play out, and then watch it come to pass.

Here is another suggestion for how you can stay vigilant and guard your mind against negative thoughts that threaten to become embedded. Put an elastic band or a stretchy bracelet around your wrist. Every time you become aware of a negative thought, take off the bracelet and move it to the other wrist. As you do that, turn the thought around. As you move the band or bracelet from one wrist to the other throughout the day, you'll stay aware of your thoughts and gradually the negative ones will diminish.

Act As If

Act as if what you do makes a difference. It does.
                                   -William James

There's one last suggestion I have for you that will make a tremendous difference in your ability to manifest massive change in your life. Act as if!

I've always been a master of make-believe. When I was a little girl it helped me to cope with some challenging life situations. I needed to make-believe that I was confident and strong so that I wouldn't be bullied. I was a prime candidate because I was small, shy, redheaded, had a strong cockney accent and was always the 'new kid'. In fact, I lived in almost thirty different homes before I was an adult.

When I was about seven—I have to admit I am rather confused about the timelines of my childhood—I ended up living in a foster home in New York City. Although I didn't know anyone, I went outside to play in the courtyard outside of the apartment building I was living in. The courtyard was all concrete and there were a lot of children, boys and girls, playing in large groups.

A bunch of boys started shooting peas at me with their pea-shooters. I was intrigued by what was hitting me and I picked one up and examined it. When I realized it was a seed of some sort, I decided to plant a garden in a little patch of ground at the edge of the courtyard. So I started egging the boys on so they would shoot me more, so that I could get a good supply of seeds to plant. I danced around in front of them and yelled, "Nah Nah, you missed me."

When I had a good supply, I planted them all in neat rows. I can't remember if they ever grew but I guess I must have given the impression that I was someone who could take care of myself because it wasn't long before I had quite the gang of little girls following me. Even then, I 'acted as if' I wasn't shy or sad, and I quickly started feeling less shy and less sad.

Of course, my skill at 'acting as if', or as it is often called, 'faking it till I made it', was an asset when I started my business and had to pretend I was an expert at anything I took on.

There's lots of evidence that 'acting as if' can result in internal changes—physical and psychological. In one study at Wake Forest University in North Carolina, a group of fifty students were asked to act like extroverts for fifteen minutes in a group discussion, even if they didn't feel like an extrovert. They found that the more assertive and energetic the students acted, the happier they became.

'Acting as if' is often used as a therapy technique for dealing with depression. Patients are instructed to go through the routines of life as though they are enjoying them even though in reality they are depressed. Initially, it may feel forced or fake, but eventually their mood starts to reflect their behaviour.

Kathy Delaney-Smith is a shining example of how to 'act as if'. When Kathy was hired as a basketball coach for a local high school over thirty years ago, she was completely inexperienced. Acting as if she was already a skilled coach, she lead the team to victory in her first year and remained undefeated for the next six years. Then, in 1998, sixteenth-seeded Harvard Women's Basketball team, with Kathy at the helm as Head Coach, battled top-ranked Stanford in the N.C.A.A. championships, and won. Stanford had one of the strongest women's programs, had won the national title twice and had a 59-game home winning streak dating back to the 1993-94 season. Harvard, on the other hand, were considered to be heavy on brains but light on athletic potential. But Harvard had Kathy and her 'act as if' philosophy.

Kathy Delany-Smith would tell her team, "Act as if you're not tired. Act as if you're confident. Act as if you're the best player because if you can do that, then you can get really and truly closer to it."

She did not allow players to show weakness even during practices. Yawning wasn't allowed. If they fell they had to get up within three seconds. She said, "We're all too busy verbalizing and saying what's wrong when we could be stronger and better if we envision what's right."

A couple of years later, Kathy had the opportunity to apply her 'act as if' philosophy again when she battled breast cancer. She learned that the human body can't tell the difference between a real event and an imagined event.

How can you apply the 'act as if' philosophy on your own path to your dream life? Incorporate acts of faith that show that you know and believe that the future that you have envisioned will show up just when it should. Behave as though you are already living the life of your dreams.

Remember when I asked you to identify those elements of your Ideal Day that you could already be bringing into your life? Are you incorporating them into the life you live right now?

Demonstrate your faith that abundance is flowing into your life by being generous and giving back or, when possible, only buying yourself the best. Don't hoard clutter. Don't wear old worn out clothes. Take extreme care of yourself and your belongings.

If you are waiting for a love relationship to show up in your life, get ready for it. Make room for it. Here's an example from Black Hat Feng Shui teachings: too often single people have their bedrooms, and their homes, set up for just one person. They have narrow beds with a bedside table and lamp on only one side. The passenger seat in the car is full of junk. They eat sitting on the couch instead of setting a place at the table. If you want a partner, get a larger bed and sleep on your own side. Put a bedside table and lamp on both sides of the bed. Clear out a drawer in the bureau for your incoming partner's clothes. Keep the passenger seat clear. Before you know it, there will be a real person right there next to you.

Think of it this way: imagine that you went to a furniture store and ordered a new couch and chair. You would immediately go home and get rid of the old furniture so that you'd be ready for the new delivery. You wouldn't wait until the delivery van drove up before preparing the space, just in case it never showed up. You have more confidence in the furniture store than that. You should have even more confidence that the Universe, your greater self, will come through for you. So now that you've created a compelling vision of the life you want to live, sent out a clear intention, and started taking inspired action, be ready when the future shows up. Act as if it already has.

In the Meantime...

Each morning when I open my eyes I say to myself: I, not events, have the power to make me happy or unhappy today. I can choose which it shall be. Yesterday is dead, tomorrow hasn't arrived yet. I have just one day, today, and I'm going to be happy in it.
-Groucho Marx

One of the challenges of using Future Pull to create the life you've always wanted is that it becomes too easy to spend all your time dreaming and not living fully in the here and now.

The expectation is that down that yellow brick road, up ahead in your perfect life, happiness is waiting for you. You begin to live a life of suspended animation, waiting to reach that place of joy and harmony. You live life on the lay-a-way plan.

That's no way to live. Right now, right here in your present, whatever that looks like, is where you can experience happiness and joy. In fact, it's essential to activating Future Pull. The energy with which you attract your future as you intend it is activated or deactivated by your emotional state. Your Future Pull power is much greater when you are happy and engaged in the life you are living in the present.

While visualizing your future exactly as you want to experience it is an important part of Future Pull, it should not be where you spend your day. Create a daily practice that includes dedicated time to visit your future life but make sure that time is short – no more than fifteen minutes. I know it's fun and exciting, but it is dangerous to spend too much time dreaming and neglecting the wonderful life that you have right now, right this minute.

Live in the moment. When you find yourself spending time in the past reliving and perhaps regretting your past, become aware of what you're doing, bring yourself back to the present moment and refocus. Don't beat yourself up about it. Treat yourself gently and guide yourself with love and patience.

Carry out each action with mindfulness and purpose. One of my teachers, James, told me how he would do simple chores with mindfulness. I've never forgotten his description of washing dishes. Because I don't have a dishwasher in my little house, I think of him each time I wash dishes. I do it mindfully. I feel the warm soapy water and let it soothe and relax my hands and arms. I take a deep breath to take in the scent of the lavender dish soap I use. I pick up each dish and wash – first its front side and then its back side – with concentration and thoroughness. Then I rinse it and place it carefully on to the rack to drain. Nothing can compete with this simple task when it comes to calming me down and helping me cope with stress. Even if you have a dishwasher, try washing a sinkful of dishes mindfully and experience it for yourself.

Express gratitude. I know I have repeated this over and over through this book. Watch for opportunities to be thankful and then express gratitude for everything you have and experience in your life.

Some days you may feel you have to reach further to find something to be grateful about. But I guarantee you this: the first may be difficult to summon up but by the time you've listed a few, you will be able to easily come up with many more.

Being grateful for the here and now is key to receiving. Allowing is about being willing to receive the blessings of the Universe as they flow to you. If you don't receive them with gratitude, the flow will stop.

Are you the kind of person that has trouble receiving gifts or compliments? Where does that come from? Do you feel you're not worthy of what you are being gifted? You are certainly worthy of all the blessings, gifts, compliments and love that come to you. Imagine if someone gave you a gift and you refused it. Gratitude, giving thanks, is an expression of love, just as much as giving the gift is an expression of love. The Universe, the source of all our blessings, is pure love. As you are one with the Universe, it is natural to express that love with gratitude.

Give more and give freely. With each chapter of this book, you have taken time to reflect or take some action to help light your path and move you along it. They have all focused primarily on you: who you want to become; what you want in your life; how you want to experience life. But never forget that as a part of the Universe, you are part of all living things. It's a trap of the ego to view yourself as separate and focus solely on yourself. Become the loving, giving person you were born to be by giving. Share love, forgiveness, happiness, laughter, ideas, growth. As you give, you keep the flow of energy moving so that you can also receive.

Have fun. Life is meant to be fun. It's an adventure. You chose to come here for the experience. Make it a great one.

This is Just the Beginning

What we call the beginning is often the end. And to make an end is to make a beginning. The end is where we start from.
                                            -T.S. Eliot

You've created a compelling vision of the life you were meant to live and started taking steps along the path to your future. Now there are several things that might happen. You may meet with surprising and unexpected miracles that quickly bring into your life exactly what you intended to manifest. Or you might start your journey and the path may roll out steadily but surely in the direction you've envisioned. But one thing is for sure: if your dream is authentically yours and you believe in it and stay focused on it, it will become reality. Then what?

The interesting thing about dreams and goals is that they are organic; they change and morph as you learn and grow. I liken it to climbing a mountain. You start off climbing with your eyes set on a point just up ahead that you can see from where you are. As you climb, your view expands and you can see further and higher. When you reach the point that you originally set as your destination, you see that there are higher, better, more beautiful points that you could climb to.

What would you do at that point? Would you sit there and feel unhappy that you didn't choose to go higher? Would you feel angry or dissatisfied because you now have to climb further to get to your new goal? Both of those reactions are possible and many people, once they've achieved a dream, feel unhappy, dissatisfied or bored because they don't know what to do next.

The first key is to enjoy the journey. If you took pleasure in the feeling of exerting yourself and successfully meeting the challenges you were faced with as you walked the path to your first destination, then setting another, higher goal will be exciting for you. The secret to enjoying the journey is to appreciate and express gratitude every day. Which of course, you do, don't you?

If you viewed your journey as a hard, slogging struggle over rocks and boulders, then the option of setting a new goal and continuing the trek will be distasteful. Once again, it is all a matter of your perception.

Either way, your journey is not over. Now that you have manifested your Ideal Day or at least brought it much closer, enjoy it. While you are living your dream life, you will be dreaming even greater dreams and setting even grander goals. It's natural to look ever higher and aspire to ever greater things.

So rest for a while and then go back to the beginning and start again. Create a new compelling vision and start taking inspired action towards your new dream.

It's what you came here to do and now you know exactly how to do it—there will be no stopping you now!

Resources

There are a variety of resources available to you at www.FuturePull.com. You can download the 'Light Your Path' pages to help you implement the tools suggested in this book.

You can also sign up to receive the Future Pull newsletter and to be informed of upcoming MasterMind Groups, Future Pull workshops and retreats. If you wish to organize a workshop or retreat in your area, you can contact me at Jackie@FuturePull.com.

If you are a member of a book club and want to make Future Pull one of your reading selections, please contact me for a discussion guide. I'd also be happy to talk to your group via Skype or teleconference to answer your questions and tell you more about some of the stories in the book.

Acknowledgements

I am very pleased to acknowledge the help of the many people who contributed their manifestation stories. During the Summer of 2010 I put out a query asking for people who had used the Law of Attraction to change their lives to contact me and share their stories. I was overwhelmed with the response and spent several months interviewing men and women from around the world. There were too many to include all the stories in this edition, but I was able to share some of them. I'd like to thank:

Alex Summer who shared his 'cosmic calendar' and his perspective on gratitude. You can read Alex's blog at http://solascendans.com

Zenovia Evans who told me the inspiring story of her triumph over a challenging childhood and youth and her success as the author of the E-book series, JD Lifeline.

Barbara Schiffman, whose book The *Exhilaration Effect: Building the Courage to Take Your Leap of Faith,* was selected as one of the top twenty-five books out of 2,800 originally submitted in the Next Top Spiritual Author competition. Her website is www.exhilarationeffect.com

Michelle Tucker who used micro-movements to take her idea for a compact, leak-proof travel accessory for women from concept to reality. Michelle is the owner of Michelle & Company. Her website is www.prettypalette.com

Edie Weinstein who told me how she persevered in her efforts to interview the Dalai Lama until she was able to realize her dream. Thank you to Edie for offering to help me make some connections so that I can knock off one of my bucket list goals—to talk to Richard Branson. Six degrees of separation is a reality in today's social networking environment. I may just take her up on that someday. Edie's website is www.liveinjoy.org

Mary Pitman who is a true entrepreneur. I think you'll be hearing about Mary's big idea soon. Thank you to Mary for sending me one of her spiritual affirmation recordings. I absolutely recommend them for night-time listening. You can find them at www.myspiritualaffirmations.com.

Deanna Lohnes for her motivational suggestions on how to get moving towards your goals. Deanna is a writer for the non-wordy and I follow her straight-talking, informative blog. Deanna's website is www.parlancellc.com or you can follow her on Twitter @DeannaLohnes.

Colleen McGunnigle who shared a real life story about using the Law of Attraction to create a clear and compelling vision of her ideal customer. Her ability to trust in the wisdom of the Universe and to allow the magic to unfold is inspiring. Colleen can be contacted at

her beautiful website
www.designbymuse.com.

I'd also like to mention Dan Falk, author of *In Search of Time: Journeys Along a Curious Dimension*. If you are interested in delving deeper into time, either on a scientific or philosophical level, go to www.danfalk.ca or www.insearchoftime.com.

About the Author

Jacqueline Garwood has created and led Law of Attraction workshops and retreats since 1989. Starting as a career coach in 1981, she became interested in helping people to take a holistic approach to life/work planning. As she began to incorporate tools such as Ideal Day and Vision Boards into her coaching and workshops, she found that people were able to change their lives in sometimes truly miraculous ways. While writing Future Pull, she interviewed people from around the world who had used these tools and techniques to manifest massive change in their lives.

Jacqueline lives in Thunder Bay, Ontario, Canada with her dog, Charlie, and cat, Kitty. Whenever possible, she travels to Ottawa to visit her son and his family. She is available for workshops, retreats and presentations. She can be contacted through her website at www.FuturePull.com.

www.ingramcontent.com/pod-product-compliance
Lightning Source LLC
LaVergne TN
LVHW051823080426
835512LV00018B/2705